"Whitney and Dwiwardani offer a uniqu
integration literature. The emphasis on cultu
that is often portrayed as an objective and rɛ
undermined by the abundant evidence of the culturally embedded and relational
nature of knowledge. The emphasis on love as the goal of integration vocationally
ties the integrative task into our common calling as followers of Jesus. Through
thoughtful questions at the end of each chapter, the authors facilitate the development of an integrative identity, which is foundational for engaging in the task
of integration."

M. Elizabeth Lewis Hall, professor of psychology at Rosemead School of Psychology,
Biola University

"*The Integration Journey* by Whitney and Dwiwardani maps on well to the
challenges many students face in relating their personal story and identity as a
Christian, their identity as a future psychologist, and the ways they want to be
responsive to matters of justice in the world today as ambassadors of Christ. I look
forward to having my students immerse themselves in it for the development of
their own integrative identity."

Mark A. Yarhouse, Dr. Arthur P. Rech and Mrs. Jean May Rech Professor of Psychology at
Wheaton College

"In a world that often compartmentalizes knowledge, *The Integration Journey* stands
as a beacon of integration, demonstrating that a deeper understanding of
Christianity can be attained by embracing the richness of our diverse human experience. Whitney and Dwiwardani have given us a gift—a guide that encourages us
to explore the relational harmony between psychology, faith, and culture. This book
is destined to become a cornerstone for those in mental health who have faith and
seek understanding."

Jennifer Ripley, Hughes Endowed Chair of Christian Mental Health Practice at
Regent University, Virginia Beach, Virginia, and coauthor of *Couple Therapy:
A New Hope-Focused Approach*

"William B. Whitney and Carissa Dwiwardani have created a personal journey of
reflection for students and psychologists. They believe that reflecting on our
personal stories within our own culture of Christian faith, psychological
understandings, and culture will lead us to an ever-unfolding wholeness. Teresa of
Avila said, 'The feeling remains that God is on the journey too.' After reading
The Integration Journey and applying it, you'll see that you've been on a journey
with God."

Everett L. Worthington Jr., Commonwealth Professor Emeritus at Virginia
Commonwealth University

"With two seasoned teachers in Whitney and Dwiwardani, I expected and found a thoughtful approach to theological and psychological reflection that is embedded in cultural contexts. But I didn't expect their generous invitation to turn this integrative meaning making inward before they empowered me to consider how to 'work toward greater love and justice in our churches, communities, and society.' Illustrated with glimpses from their integration journeys and filled with stirring questions to guide transformation, this book is a trustworthy guide to the integration journey ahead."

Joel Jin, assistant professor of clinical psychology at Seattle Pacific University and coauthor of *Deliberate Practice in Multicultural Therapy*

William B.
Whitney
and
Carissa
Dwiwardani

The
Integration
Journey

A Student's Guide
to **Faith, Culture,**
and **Psychology**

ivp
Academic
An imprint of InterVarsity Press
Downers Grove, Illinois

InterVarsity Press
P.O. Box 1400 | Downers Grove, IL 60515-1426
ivpress.com | email@ivpress.com

InterVarsity Press® is the publishing division of InterVarsity Christian Fellowship/USA®. For more information, visit intervarsity.org.

All Scripture quotations, unless otherwise indicated, are taken from The Holy Bible, New International Version®, NIV®. Copyright © 1973, 1978, 1984, 2011 by Biblica, Inc.™ Used by permission of Zondervan. All rights reserved worldwide. www.zondervan.com. The "NIV" and "New International Version" are trademarks registered in the United States Patent and Trademark Office by Biblica, Inc.™

While any stories in this book are true, some names and identifying information may have been changed to protect the privacy of individuals.

Figure 4.3: Wikimedia Commons
Figure 4.4: Photo by Bob Collier/Sygma/Sygma via Getty Images. Used by permission.

The publisher cannot verify the accuracy or functionality of website URLs used in this book beyond the date of publication.

Cover design: David Fassett
Interior design: Daniel van Loon
Images: © iMrSquid / iStock / Getty Images Plus via Getty Images

ISBN 978-1-5140-0056-4 (print) | ISBN 978-1-5140-0057-1 (digital)

Printed in the United States of America ∞

Library of Congress Cataloging-in-Publication Data
A catalog record for this book is available from the Library of Congress.

31 30 29 28 27 26 25 24 | 13 12 11 10 9 8 7 6 5 4 3 2 1

For Liam and Kaitlyn

Your excitement, smiles, and curiosity about the world

around you bring me joy every day.

WBW

To Avery and Sophia

For inspiring me to focus on the important things

and for making the content of this book real.

CD

Contents

Acknowledgments

We would especially like to thank the diverse group of students, mentors, and colleagues whose work has informed and challenged us to think more deeply about integration over the years. Your research and insights are found throughout this book, and you all have been invaluable conversation partners through your own work on integration. Thank you.

We'd also like to extend our gratitude to Pete Hill, Ev Worthington, Christina Lee Kim, Pam King, Winston Seegobin, Dave Wang, Mike Vogel, Ward Davis, Josh Hook, Andrew Shelton, Theresa Tisdale, Jennifer Ripley, and Mark Yarhouse for their early endorsements of this project. Your support and encouragement were so pivotal for us as authors and gave us valuable direction for the book.

A huge thanks to the entire team at IVP that made this project possible. Thank you so much to our editors, Jon Boyd and Rebecca Carhart, for believing in this project and offering your insights and feedback that strengthened the book at every stage. We'd also like to thank our peer reviewers, who read versions of the manuscript and offered their expertise and wisdom to make this book better.

I (William) would like to offer my deep thanks to my wonderful coauthor, Carissa Dwiwardani, for her vision, thoughtfulness, and patience throughout this writing project. Neither of us anticipated that we would be writing this book during a pandemic and during a time when our respective families were bringing kids into the world. I'm extremely grateful for your precision, creativity, and your collaborative nature that made this project immensely better at every single step along the way. Thank you for the many, many hours (and additional hours!) that you invested in this book on top of all your other responsibilities and commitments.

I'd also like to express my deep gratitude to my wife, Kimberly, for her constant love and support. During this book project she completed her doctorate in physical therapy and our two children, Liam and Kaitlyn, were born. These years have been some of the busiest but most wonderful years of my life. Kimi, your strength, wisdom, and perseverance continue to be an inspiration for me. Liam and Kaitlyn, this book is dedicated to you—thank you for constantly reminding me of God's love through the simple and beautiful way that you see the world and others.

I (Carissa) am grateful to William Whitney for inviting me on the journey of coauthoring this book. It was his vision that gave birth to this project, and his humor and friendship made the process both much more meaningful and fun. I am thankful for the many conversations we had during the writing of this book that have been personally enriching and brought clarity to the concepts in this book.

A special thanks to my husband, Anthony, for his loving support throughout the years it took to write this book. Our partnership in life, parenting, household tasks, and each other's professional pursuits has been the cornerstone of so many incredible experiences, including the completion of this project. To my daughters, Avery and Sophia, this book is dedicated to you with love and gratitude for all the ways you make the content of this book real and meaningful. I am grateful to my parents who placed the foundation of thinking and living integratively, and for their love and support throughout the years. To friends who have encouraged me on this journey, have been conversation partners, have provided feedback and recommended books, thank you.

Introduction to Integrative Reflection and Formation

*I believe in Christianity as I believe that
the sun has risen, not only because I see
it but because by it, I see everything else.*

C. S. LEWIS

About This Book

Imagine for a moment that you are going to visit New York City for the first time. Your trip is only a few days away, and with each day that passes, you can feel your excitement building. You download the New York subway app on your phone, read up on some good restaurants that you want to visit, pick out some shows that you want to see, and pack your coat because it's fall. Since your best friend from high school has moved to New York to attend university there, you've had a standing invitation to come visit. She has offered to show you New York. As your friend shows you around the city, she first of all directs you to places that are some of the must-see places to visit: the Statue of Liberty, Central Park, Times Square, and New York's Museum of Modern Art. The hope is that when you leave from your visit to New York, you will have visited some of the popular landmarks. Although your friend offers to give you a tour of New York, this doesn't mean that you will see everything that the city has to offer (since New York simply has too much to do and see during a short trip). You can't see everything on a week trip to New York, but this trip will be an introduction to the city, from the perspective of someone who can guide you to some places of interest.

The book you hold in your hands is similar to this anecdote about a trip to New York. This book, for all practical purposes, is a brief tour through the subject of how one might integrate Christianity and psychology. It is just a guide. Just as there is too much to see in a brief tour of New York, the fields of psychology and Christian theology are too vast and wide within the field of integration to sum it all up in one book. However, we must begin somewhere. That being said, not all issues regarding integration are solved, but this book provides a basic framework for understanding how to begin to reflect and practice the integration of psychology and theology together, and to form your own views on the subject. Moreover, we believe this tour of integration will be helpful for empowering our next generation of integrative thinkers and practitioners. Integration, we argue, shouldn't just be an abstract subject either. Thinking and reflecting on psychology and our Christian faith as a community from our particular cultural context will lead us into a transformative process where, over time, we are able to work toward greater love and justice.

That being said, while there are some personal parts of this tour, there is no single tour that can be completely removed from the person giving it. That's where we, your authors (Carissa and William), come in. Throughout the book we'll share some of our own experiences of integration, as well as how we think integration can be understood. Some of these views of integration are perspectives we bring to the table that you might have heard before, but others might be less familiar. However, if there's anything to learn about integration right from the beginning, it is that *you* are an integral part of the integrative process, and you have something important to bring to the integration conversation. Truth be told, we are all on a journey of becoming more integrated as people, that is, understanding how our emotions, thoughts, faith in Christ, studies in psychology, cultural identity, and actions relate to each other. Our illustration of the tour demonstrates that there's no single articulation of integration that can be separated from the person giving it, and a primary goal of this book is to help you learn more about how psychology and your Christian faith work and fit together from your particular cultural context.

Integration: The Basics

The term *integration* comes from the Latin root *integer*, which means whole or intact.[1] We use the term *integration* since we are studying both psychology and Christian theology, and we are working to reflect on them in a unified way. The question that many of our students have is: How do we think about these subjects in a unified way? And how do we move forward in thinking and reflecting about psychology and Christianity together?

We argue in this book that no real conflict exists between psychology and the Christian faith and that both can contribute to a more complete picture of the world and human person. This does not mean that there is always complete symmetry on all topics relating to our Christian faith and psychology, but it does mean

---

[1] I (William) am indebted to one of my own integration professors, Dr. Cameron Lee, at Fuller Seminary, who begins the conversation about integration by reminding students of this point.

there are considerable areas of overlap, which we as Christians must consider.

In order to be straightforward with some of our assumptions about integration, here are some key components that will guide how we approach integration in this book: (1) Integrative reflection between psychology and the Christian faith is not simply an academic exercise, or something that can be reduced to the realm of thoughts or theories. It is *embodied, lived, relational,* and *practical.* (2) Embodied integrative reflection develops over time and is part of spiritual formation and transformation. (3) Integration is always influenced by the faith background, culture, studies in psychology, and life experiences we bring to the table. (4) Practicing integrative reflection between our culture, psychology, and the Christian faith cannot be divorced from the basic principles of loving God and others. (5) Embracing and understanding our cultural and ethnic background and the cultural/ethnic story of others is an essential element of interdisciplinary work between our Christian faith and psychology. (6) Practicing integration as Christians should lead us to expand our capacities to love God and others, and should enable us to work toward greater justice in our churches, communities, and wider society.

What is integration as we understand it? *Integration is an embodied, lifelong practice of reflection and meaning-making that incorporates our Christian faith, psychology, and culture which leads to personal transformation such that we have a greater capacity to love God and others, and work toward greater love and justice in our churches, communities, and society.*

One way we can approach this process is through intentional and thoughtful reflection as a community about our own Christian faith, psychology, and particular cultural context. We believe that the first step in this transformational process is the simple recognition that *as Christians we already engage in reflecting on our faith.* Or, to roughly paraphrase the great twentieth-century theologian, Karl Barth: "You are already a theologian!" (Barth, 1981). Many times, students believe that they don't have anything to offer to the task of integration. However, as a Christian you have a basic belief in Christ, and this means you are already engaging in aspects of reflecting about your faith. Reflecting or thinking about our faith and asking how it applies to a real-life situation is the practice of theological reflection, and what theology is about. Reflecting on our faith from the particular situated context that we are embedded in (i.e., as psychology students or psychologists from our specific cultural location) is the very beginning of practicing integration for yourself.

If you are studying or interested in psychology, most likely, integration of psychology, your faith, and your culture is already occurring in your life without you even recognizing it. At first this might surprise you, but chances are you already have some beliefs or ideas about how psychology and your faith work together. Moreover, we always do this kind of reflection about psychology and our faith from our own embedded cultural context. While these beliefs and thoughts about psychology and our Christian faith might not be fully formed or articulated, they still represent some sort of beginning point for how you have already thought about psychology and Christianity. For instance, these are some common thoughts and questions we hear from our own students that represent integrative reflection on psychology, Christianity, and culture:

- "I think that counseling is about being loving toward others in a way that Jesus would."
- "I believe that God created humans, and psychology helps me understand humans better."
- "How should I understand mental illness? Is it just a diagnosis, or is something spiritual going on?"
- "In my culture, the spiritual support that people get from our church community is an important way of how my church understands well-being and thriving."

All of these statements or questions reveal some beginning thoughts or questions regarding the disciplines of psychology and Christian theology. For instance, the first statement about loving others in the way that Jesus would relates counseling and Jesus' concern for humanity, and demonstrates how a student's faith commitment helps them understand a certain aspect of psychology, such as counseling or psychotherapy.

The second statement acknowledges that psychology is studying human thought and behavior while acknowledging that humanity is God's creation (a very important point). This second statement also reveals a preliminary perspective on how psychology and Christianity should be understood together (that psychology studies humans who are ultimately created by God).

The third question reveals a potential point of tension that students commonly have. That is, what is the connection between the spiritual realm that Christianity speaks of, and the discipline of psychology that primarily includes biological and environmental explanations to mental illness? In this book, we take an integrated approach and understand that insights from psychology can be a way God helps us and provides restoration. We will unpack this more in later chapters, but foundational to the practice of integration is the belief that God works not only through a spiritual realm, such as prayers, but also through other ways, such as the help of a mental health professional.

The fourth statement recognizes the many ways that mental health, spirituality, and one's church are important from a cultural standpoint. It reveals that many different cultures understand their religious community to be an important part of psychological and spiritual well-being. We will address the importance of one's cultural identity at many different points throughout this book, but importantly from the outset, we want to stress that reflection on our Christian faith and psychology is always done from our particular cultural context.

We have heard each of these statements and questions at the beginning of the semester from students before we actually have talked about what integration is. Each of these statements reveals students have already made some connections between their own Christian faith, their studies in psychology, and their culture. But, even if you do not believe your faith has any impact on your psychology, that in itself is a theological belief or a faith statement. Some researchers within psychology believe faith does not and should not impact how we think and engage with psychology. The reality, however, is all of us have initial thoughts about our faith and psychology from our own cultural context. As mentioned above, our position assumes that (1) our faith already influences our work in psychology; (2) our work in psychology benefits from intentional theological reflection; and (3) all of this is done from the culture and context where we are embedded.

Figure 1.1 represents the three primary components of integration that we call the Integration Triad.

As you can see, the components of integration presented here are Christian theology, psychology, and culture. Integration occurs as we allow our Christian theology, our studies in psychology, and our culture to inform and transform our ideas, beliefs, and behaviors. This is represented by the overlapping circles. The place where integration occurs is actually at the overlap of all three circles. However, for ease of entering into the conversation, we can approach integration by starting at just one of the circles.

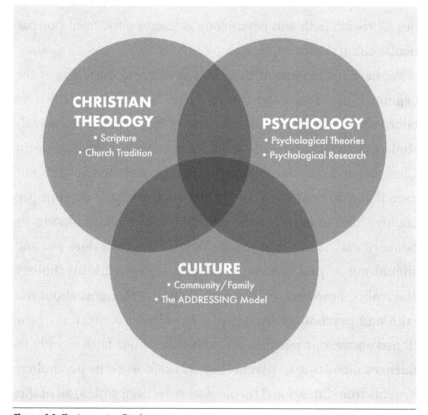

Figure 1.1. The Integration Triad

What Do We Mean When We Say "Christian Theology"?

While "Christian faith" and "psychology" and "culture" give some direction to how we understand integration, it is too broad to just speak of Christianity or psychology or culture in general. When we speak of Christian theology, we are talking about what Christians have agreed on to be the fundamentals of our faith as outlined in the Nicene and Apostles' Creeds. These creeds of Christianity uphold the importance of biblical truth provided in Scripture, and more specifically, they speak of God's good news of redemption in Jesus Christ, the redemptive purposes of God advancing in the world, and the work of the Holy Spirit that empowers us to love God and love others.

Don't let the words *Christian theology* scare you too much. One of the most famous definitions of what theology is comes from the twelfth-century theologian and Benedictine monk Anselm (d. 1109), who said that theology is *faith seeking understanding*. If we are to start from Anselm's well-known description, practicing theology is simply starting with our belief and faith in Jesus Christ, and then seeking to understand the world around us from that standpoint. This component of faith is very important because it stresses the real-life application of theology. Christian theology is (or at least always should be) involved with the world we live in— first, because God is involved with the world we live in, and second, because Christian theology always involves reflection on how Jesus Christ makes a difference to the world we live in (in this case our studies in psychology). In this book we use the words "Christian theology" and "Christian faith" interchangeably because we believe that practicing theology should be and is always connected to our faith in Jesus Christ.

In their helpful book *How to Think Theologically*, Howard Stone and James Duke (2013) alert us to the fact that first and foremost being a Christian means we are already practicing theology and have a theology. That is, we are already some degree of a theologian since theology is simply reflecting on our faith in light of the world around us. When we say that as Christians we already have a theology, we are simply noting that any statement we make about our faith or what we believe about Jesus is inevitably a theological statement. That is, it is a summary or reflection of our faith with the words we can find to describe it, as best as we can understand it at that point in time, and applied to a particular context. If we are Christian, then we inevitably already have a theology (however simple or complex it might be) and a community and culture that helped us form our faith. Consequently, whenever we think about a topic (such as psychology) from the standpoint of faith, we are engaging in theological reflection. For simplicity's sake here, we focus on the fact that theological reflection on the research and practice of psychology is, in its most basic form, what integration actually is: interdisciplinary thinking and reflection about psychology from the standpoint of our Christian faith. As we move forward, we will note that integration also involves our cultural identity, meaning-making, and transformation of who we are so that we can extend love and work toward justice.

As Christians we naturally practice theology. Any time you reflect about your faith in light of the world around you, you are engaging in some form of theological reflection from a particular context. What often begins as an everyday or working theological view of the world is developed and shaped over our lives to be more practical and applied. As we move through our lives, our theological reflection could possibly include more intentional theological training, whether that is through a local church, a community group, or a university or seminary. Our ability to think about things in a theological way and live out our faith is also enhanced and nourished by our families, churches, and communities. You probably already *do* have some thoughts about psychological topics in light of your Christian faith—you just might not recognize that you do. Chances are, as a psychology student or professional, you already engage in some aspects of thinking about how your psychology and your faith connect and relate, whether or not you are completely aware of this.

In addition, our own Christian faith is specific and contextual, in that it is informed by Scripture, particular church doctrines, and communities of interpretation (i.e., theological influences that different church denominations represent). Moreover, our Christian faith is also informed by our own cultural background and personal experiences (a very central part of our view of integration). And yours is too. For example, the way a particular church denomination practices their faith in the United States often has some differences from the way this very same denomination practices their faith in South Korea. Church traditions have rituals, rites, and values. Cultures are influenced by the community's conceptualization of God and how the divine relates to humanity. In actively conceptualizing integration as involving both theological influences and culture, the practice of integration becomes more reflective of the body of Christ in its cultural and denominational diversity. Consequently, when each of us practices integration, we are drawing on these experiences and Christian communities of interpretation that are embedded within our culture. As Brad Strawn, Ron White, and Paul Jones aptly note, the "Christian theology" part of integration is always very tradition- and experience-specific to the particular person practicing integration (Strawn et al., 2014).

What Do We Mean When We Say "Psychology"?

Psychology is the study of the human mind and behavior. According to the American Psychological Association (APA), psychology incorporates all aspects of the human experience. Psychology studies very specific things from the functions of the brain (and how this impacts our emotions and mental states), to the actions and behaviors of groups of people. Psychology also studies how people grow and change over time, examining child development or how best to care for older adults. Whether it is in scientific research centers or mental healthcare settings, understanding the mind and human behavior is what psychology is about.

Psychology also has many subdisciplines. Some of the major divisions include social psychology, cognitive psychology, neuropsychology, developmental psychology, psychology of religion, cultural psychology, and clinical/counseling psychology. In fact, the APA currently has fifty-four divisions within its organization, and each of these divisions reflects the wide variety of subdisciplines within psychology. This has caused some scholars, such as Rand Evans (1999), to refer to the current state of psychology as a "loose confederation of subdisciplines" (p. 15) under the same umbrella, since many of the subdisciplines remain so different from each other. For example, praxis-oriented psychoanalysis is quite different from the lab experimentation done with Magnetic Resonance Imaging (MRI) in neuropsychology (Evans, 1999). Although psychology is a vast discipline with many different subdisciplines, when we practice Christian faith integration with psychology, we generally practice integration by beginning from one (or several) of these psychological subdisciplines influenced by prominent researchers. Just as there are many different denominations and cultural expressions of Christianity, there are also many subdisciplines of psychology that have been influenced by key thinkers in psychology.

It goes without saying that the discipline of psychology has a tremendous amount to say about human thought, development, and behavior. Psychological research is a vital part of integration since it provides important data and research observations about the world of the human mind and behavior. Psychology is at its best when it clearly articulates these observations as measured, focused, tested, and repeatable through the use of experiments. Through the scientific method, psychology has been able to provide a great amount of empirical, factual knowledge about the world and human behavior (Bowker, 1998). The solution to any perceived tension between psychology and Christianity is to understand what science or psychology can reasonably describe and articulate. If psychologists stay within the bounds of what science can or cannot reasonably say about human behavior, then there exists no real conflict between the fields of psychology and Christianity (Plantinga, 2002). Speaking to the limits of the discipline, no one expects psychology to instruct us on matters of faith or spirituality. For instance, psychology can give us insight about religious practices of people from a social scientific perspective, discuss forms of spiritual coping, and even provide information on what forms of religious coping might be better than others, but the broad aim of psychological research is not primarily to nourish one's spiritual life. In the same way, one's faith, and in our case Christianity, doesn't provide empirical research on human behavior. When Scripture discusses human behavior, it is done from a particular perspective. There's a lot about human behavior in Scripture, but actual discussion of behavior in Scripture has more to do with how we conduct ourselves in light of God's revelation in Jesus Christ (i.e., loving God and loving others).

This just simply means that psychology provides a particular type of knowledge about human thought and behavior. More specifically for our topic here, psychology can *teach or inform us about* why humans think and act the way that they do. From an integrative perspective we have the opportunity to ask how this information from psychology helps inform or broaden our understanding of aspects of Christian theology or church practice.

What Do We Mean When We Say "Culture" and "Culturally Embedded"?

We are culturally embedded creatures, which simply means that culture always informs how we make meaning of our world. From the moment you begin to explore the world as a newborn, you do so within the context of a particular culture and context. For instance, no matter which language was spoken to you as a baby, this language was culturally embedded and carries deep cultural significance. Rites of passage in life—from birth and child rearing, to friendship, dating, and marriage, and even to grieving deaths—are all informed by cultural practices and contexts. As such, we would be remiss to write about the integration of psychology and theology without acknowledging how culture informs meaning-making (see

Bookman-Zandler & Smith, 2023; Dwiwardani & Whitney, 2022; Hoard & Hoard, 2023).

By stating that integration is culturally embedded, we also mean that the practice of integration is shaped by our cultural and ethnic backgrounds. While multicultural psychology has become a vital area of focus within the discipline of psychology since the mid-1980s (Ecklund, 2016; Pederson, 1990), discussions regarding culture and Christian theology are sometimes underrepresented within the integration dialogue (Shelton & Dwiwardani, 2022). However, more recent efforts have been made among scholars to acknowledge the centrality of culture within interdisciplinary work between psychology and Christianity.[2] In light of these developments, recognize that your cultural background is a vital part of how you practice integration. This book will help you identify different ways that you can understand both your theological tradition and cultural background as influencing how you think about your own Christian faith, and help you recognize how they all interact with the discipline of psychology.

Within integration circles, researchers have emphasized the importance of identifying one's theological location for developing integrative thinking between psychology and Christian theology (Strawn et al., 2014). At the same time, the importance of identifying our own cultural identity remains central to the enterprise of integration, since all integrative reflection between the Christian faith and psychology is done within a particular context and is influenced by our culture. For example, as

---

[2]See further Abernethy, 2012; Eriksson & Abernethy, 2014; Hook & Davis, 2012; Hook et al., 2023; Houston-Armstrong & Callaway, 2023; Jones et al., 2023; Kim et al., 2023; Pak et al., 2023; Sandage & Brown, 2018; Shelton & Dwiwardani, 2022; Whitney et al., 2023; Yangarber-Hicks et al., 2006. We'd also like to direct you to a special issue dedicated to this topic: Houston-Armstrong, T., & Callaway, K. (2023), *The Journal of Psychology and Christianity, 42* (1).

attendance in mainline Christian churches has declined over the past decades within North America and Europe (and continues to decline), Christianity has grown in Africa, Latin America, and Asia (Jenkins, 2011). This dramatic shift in the growth of Christianity means the face of Christianity in the next twenty-five years will be more diverse (less White and Eurocentric). This only adds to the relevance of culture as an essential element of integration (Kärkkäinen, 2018).

In short, culture influences our understanding of integration. The culturally embedded component of our Integration Triad reminds us that one's own theology exists only within one's own identification with gender, race, ethnicity, and nationality (and other aspects of our identity). When we practice integration, we bring all our summative life experiences about our own culture, church background, family, understanding of God, and knowledge of psychology to the table. This is what makes the task of integration an enriching experience—as well as a unique one. Your own family norms and systems, your cultural and denominational traditions, your life experiences, and your own interpretations of key aspects of Scripture will all inform your study of the discipline. In other words, we bring our own unique, embedded theological and cultural beliefs to the table when we exercise our faith and when we study psychology. The practice of integration will, therefore, be a diverse enterprise, as different aspects of culture and church tradition come to bear on how one engages the task of integration. Although there is diversity within the field of integration, Scripture provides the baseline and guide for how we understand our own experiences and how we know God through Jesus Christ.

When we speak of the culture component of the Triad, we also acknowledge that the interpretation of both Scripture and our interests in psychology are influenced by our culture, gender, family norms, faith traditions, and life experiences. Moreover, an awareness of our own cultural expressions and how these aspects of culture shape our experiences in the world is a vital aspect of spiritual development, transformation, and formation (discussed more in chapter five). Cultural and intellectual humility are also part of this transformation, since humility involves not simply tolerating the differences of others but also offering attentiveness and empathy for both oneself and others (Eriksson & Abernethy, 2014; Hook et al., 2023).

Christian Theology, Psychology, and Culture in Dialogue

Now that we have given some clarification to the terms "Christian faith" and "psychology" and "culture," we want to make it clear that we are not arguing for one specific *type* of integration. Rather, we are providing a general outline and roadmap to help you think and practice integration for yourself. Our Christian faith, our studies in psychology, and our culture inform how we practice integration. Everyone's integration journey will be unique because of the theological traditions, cultural background, and subdiscipline(s) of psychology you are familiar with.

As authors, we also cannot separate ourselves from our theological, psychological, and cultural influences as we go about interdisciplinary work between psychology and Christianity. Aspects of our cultural, theological, and family traditions always shape the way we practice integration, whether we are aware of this or not. For a brief moment, we as authors think it would be valuable to acknowledge how our theological backgrounds and culture have influenced our own integration journeys. Ultimately, our faith traditions and cultural identities matter for how we make sense of our Christian faith and what we are drawn to in the field of psychology.

I (Carissa) was born and raised in Jakarta, Indonesia, as a third-generation Christian in my family. My grandmother, who practiced animism, converted to Christianity as an adult through friendships with women in the Dutch Reformed/Presbyterian church. Growing up, she told me stories of how she used to present offerings to the spirits outside of her bedroom door before bed, so that she would be protected from evil spirits. However, when she became friends with the Christian women, she found that their kindness and friendship were so authentic and deep that she decided to become a Christian. She was baptized along with all of her children. I continued to grow up in primarily Reformed/Presbyterian churches, until I came to the United States for college. While I have attended mostly nondenominational churches in the United States, they have primarily been churches that are highly influenced by Presbyterian and neo-Calvinist thoughts, and have been the predominant influences in my interactions with integration. I also completed my undergraduate, graduate studies, and now teach at Biola University, which shape much of my thinking on integration. Ethnically and culturally, my family identifies as Chinese-Indonesian. In the United States, I am primarily identified as Asian though I never thought of myself as "Asian" growing up (since just about everyone around me was also Asian). Now having lived in two different countries, in both the West and East Coasts of the United States, and three different cities (Los Angeles area, San Francisco, and Norfolk/Virginia Beach) as a Chinese-Indonesian/Asian cisgender female, all the people I have met along the way and the meaningful conversations I had with them influence my thoughts and process in integrating Christianity and psychology.

I (William) identify as a White, cisgender, heterosexual, able-bodied male. While we'll be writing much more about ethnic and racial identity, culture, and privilege as we move through the book, for now it's important to note that these identities impact how I practice and understand integration between my faith and psychology. I'm continuing to learn ways that my White identity, privilege, and church tradition impact my views of psychology and theology. This is partly because the privileges associated with being White has the tendency to obscure the experiences of Black, Indigenous, and People of Color (BIPOC). As we will see in future chapters, our own racial identity and privilege are never side-stepped when we practice integration, but are, in fact, brought with us as we come to the integration table.

I (William) was born and grew up in Fort Worth, Texas, and my father was also born in Fort Worth, Texas, but then moved to Bartlesville, Oklahoma, when he was very young. My mother was born in Jelgava, Latvia, and then immigrated to the United States when she was about eight years old because of World War II. While Christianity has been an important part of our family for generations, it was the generosity and kindness of a Presbyterian church in Bartlesville, Oklahoma, who raised enough money to sponsor two Latvian refugees (my grandmother and mother) and provided housing and a job once they arrived in the United States. As a result of this church's kindness, both my grandmother and mother immigrated from West Germany, where they were living as refugees after their home had been destroyed by Russian forces invading Latvia. After moving to the United States, they settled in Bartlesville, Oklahoma, and attended that same Presbyterian church that had sponsored them.

The church that I grew up in Fort Worth was a Baptist church where my grandfather (on my father's side) had served as the pastor for over thirty years. I attended a Baptist university and seminary before deciding that I wanted to pursue more advanced studies in theology. Studying theology at Oxford and Fuller Seminary influenced my views of integration as I met students from all over the world from a variety of theological and cultural backgrounds. When I was in Los Angeles attending Fuller Seminary, I also worked at a Korean Presbyterian church where I served as the pastor of English ministries. Engaging in pastoral work led me to pursue a psychology degree in marriage and family therapy (also from Fuller), and I began working with clients from a variety of backgrounds at a nonprofit counseling center. Currently, I'm doing more graduate work in positive developmental psychology from Claremont Graduate University while I'm teaching psychology at Azusa Pacific University. My views of integration are still growing and expanding as I'm continually learning more in both theology and psychology through my research and teaching.

Overall though, these experiences early in my study of theology and psychology shaped some of the values I have toward culture, privilege and theological tradition, and they have helped me explore further how this impacts our understanding of integration. Consequently, my Baptist upbringing in Texas, certain interpretations of key aspects of Scripture, my theological research within the Reformed theological tradition (specifically neo-Calvinism) during my doctoral work, my experience serving in a Korean Presbyterian church as a pastor, my clinical work at the nonprofit counseling center, my time serving as a faculty member at a university with a Wesleyan heritage (Azusa Pacific University) have all informed my Christian faith, theology, and the way I think about and live out integration in my life. When I practice integration and speak about my faith, I bring all these summative experiences of spiritual formation to the table (my history, church tradition, life experiences, and White identity).

These are just a snapshot of our stories. You have one too. When we speak of Christianity, each one of us has an experience of how we came to know God and also how we became interested in psychology. Your own integration story is important to understand and reflect on since it is the intersection of God's story (Christianity) with your story. This is important not only because this makes you who you are, but because your own Christian faith is tradition-specific and is informed by particular church denominational doctrines, communities of interpretation, cultural background, and experiences.

As you can see from our own stories, Christianity has been an important part of our families' lives and our lives, and yet, we have been shaped by different cultural and theological influences. While most Christians hold to a set of fundamental beliefs consistent with the Apostles' and Nicene Creeds, Christianity is denominationally and culturally diverse. When we move toward integration with Christianity and psychology, it is necessary to reflect on what traditions, denominations, and cultures shape our understanding of our faith.

For Christians who study psychology, there are some basics such as the interpretation of Scripture that are foundational for any integrative task. For instance, each of us understands God and values science, and we make meaning of both our faith and science through different cultural communities that aid us in interpretation. Our own cultural communities help us read, understand, and interpret Scripture, in that we are always situated within a specific context. We also have communities that help us learn about and make sense of psychology (this mainly happens through our classes and coursework). Consequently, this book is not just about you learning all of the information here, but also about you coming into contact with parts of your own faith and culture and inquiring how these impact the specific aspects of psychology you are already studying.

Given that, the overarching goal of this book is to provide you with an integration roadmap that helps you understand the basic landscape of integration. This will be done by helping you think about psychology, your faith, and culture all together, and helping you practice integration from your particular faith and cultural tradition. It's okay if you are not familiar with all of the traditions of your faith. Through Scripture we have witnessed God's gracious interaction with humanity and the world through Jesus. Each of the major Christian traditions will attest to this fact, and while there are theological disagreements to how some aspects of Scripture are interpreted, we believe that theological diversity adds to the richness of the integration dialogue, rather than taking away from it. Moreover, we also argue that cultural diversity adds to the richness of the integration dialogue and is an essential part of it.

While Christianity and psychology are not always in agreement, they are not always in conflict either. At many points psychology and Christianity can work quite well together and even clarify the other to give us a broader and richer picture of reality. It is that picture of reality, informed by Christian faith and psychology, that we invite you into as we move forward.

Our students commonly ask: How do I actually practice integration for myself, and what exactly are we doing? These are excellent questions that will be answered over the course of the book, but we will begin addressing this question in this chapter. Perhaps you have had similar types of questions as you have thought about the subjects together. While we do want students to be able to think about how psychology and Christianity work together, the integration of the disciplines is a much more dynamic process that goes beyond just thinking about the concepts of psychology and Christianity. We also believe that integrative thinking further includes being shaped and transformed by the integrative process itself. Or, as Steven Sandage and Jeanine Brown (2018) have aptly stated, integration has a vital interpersonal and relational component to it, since it is people who are practicing integration. We support their relational approach.[3] Consequently, we are not approaching integration as the interplay of abstract ideas that are separate from our own embodied lives and stories—for example, our Christian tradition, cultural, and racial identity (Sandage & Brown, 2018). As you will see, integration requires

---

[3]You will find that aspects of this book align with some of the major themes in Sandage and Brown's (2018) book, *Relational integration of psychology and Christian theology: Theory, research, practice.* As authors, we are indebted to Drs. Steven Sandage and Jeannine Brown for their research, and agree with their approach, as well as agreeing with other approaches to integration that are embodied, practical, relational, and lead to deeper reflections on cultural identity, love, and justice.

thoughtfully reflecting on your experiences within psychology, your culture, and your faith, in addition to consciously committing to practice and live out your life in an integrated way.

The argument of this book is that integration primarily occurs as we begin to make meaning of our faith, psychology, and culture. Our views on integration develop and are shaped as we live our life and encounter new situations that cause us to reflect on our Christian faith, psychology, and culture in new ways (described further in chapters five and six). Thinking about or reflecting on your faith, psychology, and culture is a practice that can be taught—but it is also a practice formed within us through conversation, sharing of stories, and hopefully some fun along the way too. (Okay—not Disneyland kind of fun, but the kind of fun that comes with knowing, growing, and becoming more self-aware.) Humans are fascinating creatures, and God made us both curious and complex. While this book is not the final word on the process of integration, we outline here the important and foundational guidelines regarding how one should approach particular aspects of psychology (e.g., neuroscience, social psychology, research methods) in a way that is theologically informed. Moreover, in this book we advocate for owning our own stories within Christianity, psychology, and culture.

Sometimes in our classes there are some students who think there is no relationship between the subjects at all, and sometimes we find a number of students who think there is no conflict between psychology and the Christian faith but aren't sure how they fit together. These viewpoints are valuable since they still represent starting points for how you understand the relationship between your Christian faith, psychology, and culture. Integration is a process, and we each exist at different places when we begin the process. In many ways, the process of reflecting on theology, psychology and culture is about employing the different resources that are part of our cultural background, faith traditions, and experiences. Or said another way, practicing integration for ourselves begins when we use those resources we embody and the resources we are embedded in to reflect on how those very resources might come to bear on our research and practice within the discipline of psychology.

Wrapping Things Up

This book is to help you think about and practice integration in a way that is theologically, psychologically, and culturally informed. Integration continually changes as we grow and develop—as we learn more about the world around us, deepen our own spiritual and faith commitments, and further our studies in psychology. As folks who do research and clinical practice in the field of integration, our goal is to help you develop and grow in your faith as you understand more deeply the relationship between your faith, cultural background, and studies in psychology. For the Christian, the integration of psychology and theology is being able to give an answer for how our faith relates to psychology in addition to living out both love and justice in the particular context where we are placed.

Reflection Questions

As we begin this journey, we have some brief reflection questions for you that will help you think along the three major components of the Integration Triad.

1. As best as you can at this time, how do you understand the relationship between your Christian faith and psychology? Make a list of four to five ways you see that they relate.

2. In the first question above you listed ways the Christian faith and psychology might be related. Are there any ways that you might perceive them to be in conflict? Write down two to three ways that come to mind.

3. Think now about your own cultural background (for now just think about your own racial and ethnic identity). How does your cultural background influence your faith? How might it influence your studies in psychology?

Integration as Story

*There is no greater agony than bearing
an untold story inside you.*

MAYA ANGELOU

*Life must be understood backward;
but . . . lived forward.*

SØREN KIERKEGAARD

During my twenties, I (William) worked with a lot of church youth groups. Typically, this work involved helping out at weekend church retreats for junior high and high school students. Most of these retreats were focused on spiritual growth, however, they also had a good amount of social and fun activities built into the schedule. In what follows, I will share one of the experiences I had, and as a warning, the following story may bring up difficult emotions due to references to death and suicide. If you feel that you'd prefer not to read the rest of the story, feel free to jump to the next section.

One year, I was helping with one of these church retreats, and was placed as a leader of a small group of junior high boys. While there were lots of other leaders at this particular retreat, my main job was to form relationships with this group of junior high boys and lead them in multiple Bible studies over the course of the weekend. If you've ever been to one of these church retreats, you know you can grow surprisingly close to each other in the short period of a weekend. Youth often share vulnerably and honestly about how they are really doing and what is going on in their lives.

On one of the last nights of this particular retreat I was leading, these junior high guys had really been supportive of each other and had talked about some of the difficulties they were facing both at home and at school. At the end of this last small group time for the weekend, one of the boys asked if he could speak to me privately about something he didn't feel comfortable sharing with the group. Of course, I told him I'd be happy to talk with him, but I remember feeling nervous about what this private topic might be.

As we talked, he shared about a difficult home life and sadness he had been feeling for a long time. He also told me that earlier in the previous week he had been so sad and hopeless that he could not see the point in living anymore. As he talked, I could hear the distress in his voice and see the pain in his face. He described to me why he believed there was no other way out of this feeling of being trapped and sad except to kill himself. Since he felt so trapped, lonely, and hurt, he had started making a plan to end his life about a month ago.

He had been over at a friend's house many times, and knew where his friend's dad kept his shotgun and where his friend's father hid the shotgun shells. He had made sure to visit this friend's house earlier in the week. While his friend was busy playing video games, he had quietly sneaked the shotgun and a box of shotgun shells out of the house. He took the shotgun and shells back to his own bedroom, hid them, and planned to die by suicide later that night. Late that evening with the shotgun loaded, he prayed to God one last time for help before he pulled the trigger. But at that moment, something strange happened. He was overcome with a deep sense that God was telling him to stop immediately. The message was clear: Stop what you're doing and go to your friend's church retreat this weekend and talk to someone.

At this point I understood why his desire to talk with me was so urgent. This was a cry for help, even though he would never have said it that way. As I think back to this experience, I remember feeling such empathy for him since he was hurting so badly. It was excruciatingly painful to know that the only option he felt he had was to end his life. I remember asking him if he had talked about this with his youth pastor or anyone else at the church. He said he had, and I immediately felt a bit of relief.

"What did they say or do to help you with this?" I asked. But the relief I previously felt for a moment, thinking that others were actively helping him, quickly melted away. "Oh, they did try to help. I even talked to the pastor. When I told the pastor I wanted to kill myself, he told me that I needed to pray more and that he would be praying for me."

As a twenty-year-old with no mental health training, I didn't know exactly what to do in this situation. I did know several things though. First, this boy needed more help than what had previously been given and more help than I could give him. Second, I was in shock that, at least as he told the story, this was all that had been done by the pastor and youth leader. I knew the advice to "pray more" wasn't going to cut it in this case, and some other more intentional intervention was needed. Over the next few days, we were able to get this boy more help, but I've been haunted by this early experience that lies squarely in the intersection of psychology and faith integration.

Don't get me wrong. There are many churches that do a fantastic job of dealing with mental health issues, but I've also encountered a lot of churches along the way where only a spiritual solution was provided (e.g., "pray more") when more action was needed. In these cases the most spiritual solution is to get more intentional support from a trained mental health professional, or if it is an emergency, call 911. The problem is that many pastors and church leaders don't have training to know when someone needs to be referred, or often don't have a framework for understanding how some mental health issues should be handled. I also believe that churches can help with this process, but often they don't have a clear picture of how they should speak into issues of mental health. Some of this is also practical. Pastors often get a lot of training, but they can't be trained in everything. Some research shows that in times of psychological distress, individuals with religious affiliations seek help from religious leaders more readily than from trained mental health professionals (Wang et al., 2003). For many, the pastor or church leader is frequently the one consulted when a religious person reaches out for help (Chalfant et al., 1990).

My encounter with this junior high boy was one of my first experiences where I began to reflect more intentionally on how my Christian faith was related to psychology. What I didn't know at the time was that I was beginning to reflect theologically on what was going on with this boy and how to best get him help. In fact, the conclusion I drew from this experience (i.e., God works through both prayer and professional mental health care) was how I began to understand my initial ideas about faith and psychology. This early experience also informed why I believe the integration of faith and psychology is important. Many Christians can benefit from understanding that God can use mental health care to help bring healing.

The story above also highlights how we carry implicit assumptions about how psychology relates to the Christian faith and vice versa. Whether you recognize it or not, you already engage in what we might call some beginning aspects of theological reflection about psychology from your own cultural context. One of the most fundamental elements in practicing integration is the acknowledgment that, no matter where you are on your journey as a Christian, you already have some initial thoughts regarding Christianity and psychology. We are interested in finding out what these initial reflections are, since we believe that these initial thoughts are your beginning stages of integration that incorporate your faith, psychology, and culture. For instance, when I first talked to this boy, I had no formal mental health training, but I did have some initial ideas on how to respond, which involved spiritual guidance but also professional mental health help. When we understand integration as a process that progresses over time, we better understand that we all begin somewhere, and as we further study and reflect on our own stories, we grow in our integration journey.

Owning Our Untold Stories

Søren Kierkegaard, the famous Danish philosopher, explains another element of one's life story, and how the many aspects of our "storied" lives are not immediately understood in the movements themselves, but only in retrospect, in hindsight. Simply put, we live our life in the here and now, but we don't often understand or make meaning of our life until we look back and reflect on it.

You might ask what owning our story and reflecting on our story has to do with psychology and the Christian faith. Quite a lot, actually. Christians over the centuries have always believed that God actively guides and directs our life story. Our thought life, mind, body, biology, and personality are all factors that contribute to make you the unique person you are. Or as award-winning author Brené Brown describes it, we are both "biology and biography" (Brown, 2012). As humans we are the biological components of body and mind together, but the storied experiences of our biography make up a huge aspect of who we are. As we turn toward integration, we will get in touch with the parts of our story that impact various parts of our spiritual lives, our experiences, and our culture. We start where we are, and then look backward to understand ourselves better.

Our views of integration continue to develop over a period of time. Your faith continues to develop and change as you encounter different experiences and grow older. Your knowledge and awareness of your own cultural identity grows and develops over our lives as you have new experiences, and you reflect on your own cultural story. As you progress through your psychology courses and encounter different life experiences, your views of integration will also change, develop, and grow in complexity. However, we all begin somewhere with initial ideas or thoughts about our faith, psychology, and culture. While we all begin somewhere, we hopefully continue to develop our views of integration, and live or practice integration within our day-to-day lives.

As Neff & McMinn (2020) correctly note, "Each of us brings a story to the task of integration and those stories influence our ways of understanding God, ourselves, the world around us, and the work we do in counseling and psychotherapy" (p. 9). As authors, we appreciate and affirm this focus. That's why in this chapter, we will develop this theme of *story* by helping you reflect on your own stories, and providing more detail on how integration can be understood as a story that develops over time. In our last chapter, we introduced the three components of the Integration Triad: Christian theology, psychology, and culture. In this chapter, we will focus on the Christian theology and psychology elements of our stories, and we will focus on the culture aspects of our storyline in chapter four. While we all begin with some initial integrative ideas about our faith, psychology, and culture, these ideas continue to grow and change (i.e., develop) as we learn more, reflect more, and have different experiences within the particular context and culture that we find ourselves in. Our hope is that this chapter will help you write and reflect on your own integration story, by looking at different aspects of our identity from the perspective of your Christian faith, psychology, and culture.

 Key Concept 2.1

We develop our integrative views and identity as we reflect on the various stories that make up our own lives from our Christian faith, psychology, and culture.

As Christians, we believe that the primary story of our life should be shaped by Christ. At the same time, when we really consider how we come to think and believe what we do, our faith is shaped and formed in the contexts and communities that we find ourselves in. Two people whose lives are shaped by Christ could come to think about integration from different perspectives and both bring something that enriches the kingdom of God, making a real-world difference. In addition to our own Christian story and relationship with God, we are also shaped by what we learn in the sciences (psychology), and our own ethnic, cultural background, and family traditions (culture).

While we gave a brief description of what we mean when we speak of Christian theology and psychology in our last chapter, what follows will provide some more guidance to how our theology and psychology relate to each other. Christianity has never been a

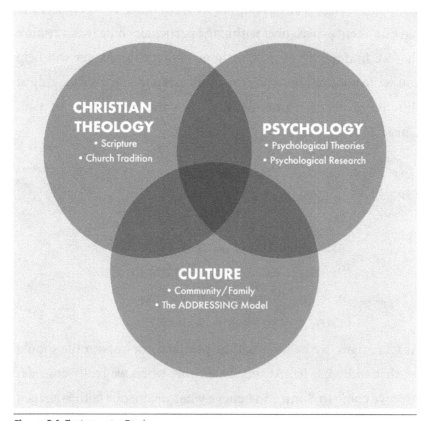

Figure 2.1. The Integration Triad

monolithic belief system without texture and color. Most Christians agree on certain beliefs, yet our culture, experience, and denominational and family traditions are all incorporated into how we understand Christianity. Still, as Christians, we all agree that the story of God interacting in the world through the Spirit of Christ holds a special place of importance, and operates as an overarching narrative that shapes and guides all other stories.

Moreover, psychology is also not a monolithic discipline, as our understanding of it is largely shaped by the focus of our study within the various subdisciplines of psychology. Psychology, like Christianity, also has a tradition, history, scientific culture, and spectrum of views and beliefs within the discipline. While the tradition of psychology is different from that of Christianity, it has a tradition nevertheless. As we think of psychology, for example, those studying to be clinicians will naturally have a clinical focus to their story of learning within psychology, while for those studying cognitive psychology, there will be a focus on how mental structures shape perception, memory, and learning in their study of psychology. The subdiscipline we study within psychology shapes and forms us. This results in our looking at the situations as students of psychology with slightly different psychological lenses, ones that are often informed by the particular subdiscipline of psychology we have spent the most time studying.

In a similar way, when we consider culture as one of the stories that informs our lives, we consider our own race/ethnicity, but also other aspects of our culture that we identify with, and how these various identities intersect and influence our growth and development currently and over time (Hays, 2008; Hunt, 2001). In fact, one's culture cannot be set aside as we practice integration, and we argue that our inhabited cultural background and stories of our lives are the concrete realities where we begin to actually practice integration. We can never step outside our own skin, culture, or context, and yet, we *can* continually become more reflective and grow in our own cultural awareness.

It is also valuable to note, however, how much the waters we swim in are unnoticeable to us. A clinical psychologist might not know exactly how a cognitive psychologist would view a mental disorder like depression, because her focus has been on the clinical side of treating depression. Or a Methodist might not know what Catholics believe about the sacraments because he grew up Methodist, and he only knows what Methodists believe about Communion. Or we might not have considered how our cultural identity influences how others treat us because we have certain privileges that are invisible to us.

Scottish philosopher Alasdair MacIntyre argues that we can only answer the question of how we should act or be in the world by first answering the question: What kind of stories am I a part of? (2007). Each of these elements (Christian theology, psychology, culture) listed above has a formative role in shaping our lives. Sustained reflection on these stories helps us make meaning of them in a new way. One aspect of our own faith development, MacIntyre argues, is to become more aware of the traditions in which we are embedded (2007). All of us inhabit storied traditions, and by becoming more aware of the traditions we inhabit, we are able to use the formative texts of our tradition (Scripture) and learn how to apply them to the current context where we exist (both our own cultural context and our studies in psychology; Murphy, 2018).

Or, to use Hans-Georg Gadamer's (1975) terms, we all have a historically situated (or historically effected) "consciousness"

(p. 237) that we inhabit (Callaway & Whitney, 2022). Thus, practicing integration between Christian theology, psychology, and our cultural context involves recognition of our historical situation, examination of the cultural traditions that we inhabit, reflection on the science of psychology, and reflection on formative texts of Scripture. Becoming more aware of the stories and traditions we inhabit is a key component for how we understand integration and the development of our own integrative identity. There will always be difficulties in trying to apply one's faith tradition to the current context, and there will always be individual differences and diversity among persons as we become more aware of the stories we inhabit. However, MacIntyre also reminds us that an essential feature of embodying a tradition like Christianity is striving to resolve difficulties within the tradition to chart a way forward. We, as authors, see that the integration community is doing just this—staying engaged and continuing to reflect and resolve difficulties within our own integration tradition of thinking about psychology and Christianity together (MacIntyre, 2007).

One additional point should be made here about our storied lives. Notre Dame sociologist Christian Smith has been careful to note how our human narratives have a formative component. While we do inhabit narratives (MacIntyre) and have a historically situated consciousness (Gadamer), it's just as important to understand that narratives shape and direct our lives (Smith, 2003). Smith says it like this:

> [We are] *made by* our stories. We tell and retell narratives that themselves come fundamentally to constitute and direct our lives. We, every bit as much as the most primitive or traditional of our

ancestors, are animals who most fundamentally understand what reality is, who we are, and how we ought to live by locating ourselves within the larger narratives and metanarratives that we hear and tell, and that constitute what is for us real and significant. (Smith, 2003, p. 64)

For Christians who study psychology, the guiding narrative for our lives is our Christian narrative given in Scripture—the guiding narrative of God's revelation of God's own self through Jesus Christ. Even those who do not claim to be religious or spiritual still have a narrative (or multiple narratives) that guides their life. This may be a capitalist progressive narrative (where capitalism's wealth is the source and solution for social mobility and happiness) or a scientific Enlightenment narrative (where we can ease suffering and solve problems in the world through science). No matter who we are though, as humans we inhabit narratives and are shaped by these narratives (Smith, 2003). As a result, we should always become more aware of the dominant narratives shaping our lives and recognize that the meaning we make of our own story of our Christian faith, psychology, and culture will become an integrated narrative that actually gives shape and meaning to our own life.

Taking this theme of narrative and meaning-making in a uniquely Christian direction, James K. A. Smith correctly points out that we are creatures shaped by our Christian worship and liturgies (i.e., our practices) because we are creatures fundamentally shaped by what we love (Smith, 2009). This practice of love (given by God through Jesus Christ) is extremely important for how we understand integration, and necessary for the future of integration to have a distinctly formative component.

All of this simply highlights the importance of the narratives that we are going to further discuss in this book, how these narratives give our lives meaning, and how they shape and form us as people. Moreover, as we reflect on our Christian theology, our culture, and the discipline of psychology, we locate the various elements that shape our viewpoints and life in different ways. Please note that while some sustained reflection enables us to draw out threads and classify distinct domains as Christian theology, psychology, or culture, the place where we live our actual lives is in an intersection of all of these domains. It is in looking backwards, as Kierkegaard notes, that we begin to make meaning of our cultural identity, Christian theology, and interests in psychology. Moreover, we don't always realize all the influences that shape our lives as we are living through them. It is only thoughtful reflection while looking backwards that helps us make sense of our experience. This reflection and sustained attention to these stories helps us develop as persons who live integrated lives.

Reflection on the stories in our lives is organic and begins where we are. It is an approach that honors the familial stories, cultural stories, and spiritual stories that we already inhabit. In other words, it is a bottom-up approach of reflecting on these three components of the story of integration (as opposed to being top-down, abstract, or theoretical). However, it does not stop there. Neff and McMinn (2020) also remind us about the importance of dialogue and conversation as key parts of integration, and they acknowledge that this work on understanding our own stories and meaning-making becomes more clear as we do it in community with others. In dialogue, we often become more aware of the stories which inform our approach to integration. Further, in dialogue, we may encounter the opportunity to critically evaluate where we are and take steps toward further development in our integrative process.

Many factors could prompt a sustained study and reflection on our stories. For example, we have an experience that requires something different from us or causes us to embody life differently. The event that precipitates our reflection could be mundane, jarring, or anywhere in between. On the more jarring end of the continuum, it could be a life crisis, a loss, or a national tragedy. On the more day-to-day end of the continuum, it could be a class discussion, a conversation with a mentor or friend, or participating in a cultural event.

Key Concept 2.2

Within the Integration Triad, the Christian theology storyline speaks of our own faith, which is shaped by Scripture and church tradition.

The first domain that we will discuss more is Christian theology. This is the story of God's interaction with humans and the world. Scripture and church tradition are two components that give this story its shape and direction. Practicing Christian theology means we seek to understand God's story revealed to us in Jesus Christ. However, practicing theology also means that we seek to understand the world around us from the standpoint of our faith in Jesus Christ *and* embody practices that extend God's love and justice in a particular context to bring wholeness and healing. Theologians Miroslav Volf and Matthew Croasmun (2021) similarly note that the purpose of theology is to "discern, articulate, and commend visions of the flourishing life in light of the person, life, and teachings of Jesus Christ" (p. 45). Thus, the practice of our theology always includes the action components of living out our faith in the world around us and of applying our faith to a particular context. One's own faith beliefs are always informed by Scripture and communities of interpretation (i.e., our church) and applied to a specific context that we find ourselves in as Christians. Since Scripture has the primary role in shaping our Christian narrative and faith, it will help to say a few things about it here.

Scripture. In the late fourth century, the North African bishop Saint Augustine of Hippo reminded his readers to adhere to certain guidelines when reading Scripture. In his work *On Christian Doctrine* (AD 397), Augustine taught that all interpretations of Scripture should ultimately lead and guide its readers toward love of God and love for other people. As Augustine notes, if we forget that the purpose of interpreting Scripture is encountering God and God's love in Christ, then we run the risk of reading the Scripture incorrectly. Augustine's point is that many people can read Scripture, but the person who is actively loving God and loving neighbor will read Scripture differently from the one who is not (Strahan, 2012). And if Augustine could speak to our present-day faculty or students who are Christians and studying psychology, he would remind us that many people can practice or engage in the task of integration of psychology and Christian theology, but the person who is actively loving God and loving neighbor will practice integration differently from the one who is not.[1] This one simple

---

[1]You also might find it noteworthy that Augustine believed that our theology always needed to be in conversation with the best science available at the time. He argued that Christians needed to know about their faith, but also be knowledgeable of science in order to engage in a way that was intellectually viable (or reasonable) with those who were not Christians.

but profound point about directing our love toward the certain end goal, or *telos*, of loving God and neighbor will ultimately mean our understanding of integration is inherently spiritual and transformational (Smith, 2009). In fact, this point about both love and transformation is the major component of Coe and Hall's (2010) integrative approach in their work *Psychology in the Spirit*, where they argue that psychology can actually be seen as an act of loving God and neighbor.

This interpretive principle of love is extremely helpful as we practice integration, since it will guide us if we feel lost or confused along the way. Thus, reading and interpreting Scripture are not just intellectual games or puzzles, not merely something to be read in order to debate, and certainly not something that can simply be used as a resource to inform psychology or our culture and then put to the side. Instead, we must understand that reading Scripture is for knowing and relating to God, opening ourselves to Christ's love, and being transformed by God's Spirit. This makes Scripture reading vital to the integrative process. Prayer makes a difference in this process too. A simple prayer asking God to speak and help us be open to listening is always a wonderful way to direct our study, learning, and reflection. Saint Benedict's (ca. AD 516) first rule of being a disciple was to listen, and Saint Benedict encouraged his own readers to listen to how God's voice was calling them to pray, have faith, and do good in the world around them.

All Christians will agree that Scripture informs, shapes, and transforms how we understand God, our own self and place in the world, and other people and relationships. Scripture never floats free and lands objectively on people's laps where it is understood in the same way by everyone. All Scripture is read or heard, and then we make sense of what is read or heard. That being said, all Scripture is interpreted from a particular context. These interpretations of Scripture, and our emphasis on certain aspects of some Scriptures over others, largely depend on how our church communities and other cultural communities have helped us make sense of the text.

Scripture is our guide, but keep in mind that we also read and interpret aspects of Scripture from the particular church tradition and culture where we find ourselves. For instance, when I (William) was a kid, I spent concentrated amounts of time reading Psalms. I liked reading them because of the honesty and emotion that was expressed toward God. I also felt like they encapsulated some of my own experiences and longing. Then for a couple of months when I was ten, our pastor did a sermon series on Psalms. Some of the psalms that I was familiar with came alive in a new way as I understood the background and context of what was going on in the life of David. These sermons enhanced my understanding and interpretation of these psalms, and changed the way I read them— for the better! This is an example of how our church communities help us make sense of or read a text. The background knowledge I gained through that sermon series helped me read and interpret other psalms.

In addition to the guiding principle of love, all reading of Scripture involves *crosscultural conversation*. Reading Scripture is always a crosscultural conversation because the culture of the Bible and the culture of our contemporary world are undeniably different. However, whether we recognize it or not, we read and interpret Scripture at the intersection of these cultures, our culture and that of the Bible. Anytime any of us reads Scripture, we engage in a crosscultural conversation as we enter into the culture of the Bible from our own specific cultural location. To do this well, we must acknowledge the same Holy Spirit working in the ancient world and in our contemporary world has been speaking to our mothers, fathers, grandmothers, grandfathers, sisters, and brothers in the faith to lead, guide, sustain, and shape communities in the way of Jesus Christ (Green, 1997; Strahan, 2012).

This crosscultural conversation between the world of the Bible and the culture of our day is the intersection where we make sense of what Scripture means. New Testament scholar Scot McKnight notes that reading Scripture involves an ongoing adaptation to new conditions of the modern reader (McKnight, 2018). This simply means that no reading of Scripture stays locked in the world of the Bible. Rather, we seek to make sense of it and apply it to our current situation. Reading Scripture in an integrative fashion means that we will naturally make connections to the context and other communities of interpretation that we inhabit. For integrative reflection between psychology and our Christian faith, this means that we will read Scripture and naturally make connections with psychology, since our studies in psychology represent a context and community that we inhabit. To be good interpreters of Scripture, we must recognize that we cannot always make direct moves from Scripture to psychology, but we can understand how certain parts of Scripture can inform our psychological views (Simundson, 1989).

Consequently, as Daniel Migliore reminds us, traditional Western (and predominantly White) interpretations of the person and work of Christ are no less cultural or contextual than those done by African American theologians or by women (Migliore, 2004). Cultural history and context also influence the various ways we read Scripture and understand Christ's work of salvation and restoration. Renowned scholar and theologian James Cone has highlighted how the history of slavery in America provides a backdrop that makes certain passages of Scripture hold great importance for African Americans (Cone, 2012b). An example of this would be the exodus story of the Israelites being enslaved and then being freed from slavery. Cone reminds us reading the exodus narrative about the Israelites as slaves in Egypt will feel different if you had ancestors who were enslaved or oppressed (Cone, 2011; 2012b).

While our culture influences how we understand certain parts of Scripture, we also must remember to listen to what God is saying to us through the Scripture. God communicates with humanity about God's own self, God's work in the world, and salvation through Jesus Christ in the pages of Scripture. Scripture also teaches us about God's Spirit who empowers us and is working to restore and bring wholeness to creation. In fact, the Bible is God's story of encounters with humanity over a period of time among a certain people (Israel) with a culture, history, and heritage. The Bible is not God, but God uses the Bible and speaks through the Bible. God wants to encounter us through Scripture, and God's Spirit is with us and guides us.

In the Protestant tradition, there is a strong Reformation focus on reading Scripture for ourselves, but even luminaries in the Protestant tradition like Luther and Calvin stressed that Christians shouldn't read the Bible without guidance, or read Scripture in complete isolation (McKnight, 2018). In fact, many streams of American Christianity have dangerously promoted hyperindividualism to the point that we have forgotten about the nearly two thousand years of writing and communal tradition that our present-day faith draws on. We must also soberly consider that a good number of historians note that White Christianity's individualistic views of salvation contributed to many White Christians being silent about racial injustices in the United States (Jones, 2020). We will expand on this point more in chapter four on culture. In the next section, we will turn our focus to the role of tradition in Christian theology.

Church tradition. If you reference the Christian theology circle in figure 2.1, you'll see that it includes Scripture (which we just described) and church tradition. When we talk about church tradition, we are referring to the various communities of interpretation in our current time and over the centuries. Scripture is never read in isolation, and it should never be interpreted in isolation. Worldviews and values that have been shaped in our storied lives play a part in how we read and interpret Scripture, and many of these templates are inherited from our culture, local church communities, and the traditions and practices of the church over time. Think for a moment about some of the most important practices of your church, like baptism or the Eucharist (a.k.a. the Lord's Supper). The way these sacraments are practiced likely did not emerge from your local church, but was inherited and shaped by a long tradition of church history over time (yes, even if you say your church is nondenominational). Our Integration Triad recognizes that there are two additional components that make up one's church tradition: (1) ancient church tradition and (2) denominational and local community traditions.

Ancient church tradition, or the "Great Tradition," as Scot McKnight (2018) calls it, is based on the fundamentals of our faith informed by ancient Christian wisdom (such as the Nicene Creed or the Apostles' Creed) and the sacraments (like baptism and the Eucharist). For instance, the Nicene Creed was adopted in AD 325 by the Council of Nicaea and remains an important summary of the Christian faith that nearly all Christians have relied on throughout the centuries. As the church encountered controversies and challenges, certain aspects of the creed were updated or added to by the Second Ecumenical Council held in the city of Constantinople in 381 (now Istanbul in modern-day Turkey). Both of these creeds solidified how the church thought about the divinity of Jesus Christ and laid the groundwork for how the church thought about the doctrine of the Trinity. No matter what Christian tradition you align with (Catholic, Orthodox, or Protestant), all Christian traditions draw on these early creeds to inform their basic conceptions of faith. In fact, even after the Great Schism between Eastern Orthodox and Roman Catholic in 1054, the church in the West remained predominantly Catholic. This changed in 1517, when a young Catholic priest named Martin Luther nailed his Ninety-Five Theses on the church door at Wittenberg, ultimately starting what is now known as the Protestant Reformation. Other denominations such as Anglican, Methodist, Baptist, Presbyterian, Church of Christ, and many others emerged after 1517.

While there are many other examples of ancient church tradition, the creeds are one example that all Christians draw on. This ancient tradition is cumulative interpretations, rituals, teachings, writings, and customs of the church that have been passed down to us over time (Stone & Duke, 2013). Whether we recognize it or not, all Christian denominations rely to some degree on this wisdom of the past, and we would be remiss not to acknowledge the role that this ancient tradition plays in contemporary Christianity.

In addition to ancient church tradition, our own church denomination and traditions of our local church community also influence how we understand our Christian faith. Again, it is important to realize that denominations don't just pop up fully formed from nowhere. They are often the result of movements that start from within another denomination or stream of Christian thought. For instance, Martin Luther, who spearheaded the Protestant Reformation in 1517 and founded the Lutheran denomination, was a Catholic monk and priest. Luther's movement was intended to reform the Catholic church (which is where we get the word *Reformation*). When Luther started speaking out against the Catholic church, he never intended to break away from the Catholic church, only to reform some of its practices that he didn't see fitting with Scripture. Or consider John Wesley, who was a priest within the Anglican Church (a.k.a. the Church of England). The Methodist denomination began as a revival movement within the Anglican Church after Wesley experienced his "heart strangely warmed" at the church in Aldersgate, London, in 1783.

Our point here is that even some of the luminaries in our Protestant history gave birth to theological movements because of their context. We also have a context and history where we have interpreted Scripture in, and because many of us are in the United States, this context involves certain racial and cultural dynamics that are unique to the United States. William Dyrness notes that among White Christians in America during the twentieth century, it was mainly only missionaries and crosscultural evangelists that gave any thought to a theology of race and ethnicity (Dyrness, 1997). This is despite the fact that the United States has a long history of slavery and racial segregation. As a result, the story of your particular denominational tradition is incredibly important, especially how it intersects with your ethnic and racial identity. In other words, considering the cultural aspect of our stories is such an important part of becoming more integrated as people. While the examples above illustrate how denominations arise from streams of previous Christian thought, it's most important to recognize and acknowledge the particularities of your own denomination and influences shaping your local church tradition. This shapes the way we read and interpret Scripture, and emphasizes certain aspects of Christian belief within Scripture.

Brad Strawn, Ron Wright, and Paul Jones (2014), in their work "Tradition-Based Integration," have accurately brought to light how Christianity cannot be thought of as a monolithic system under the term *Christianity*. Everyone's understanding of Christianity has contours and particularities of traditions and denominations that are embedded within their Christian belief system. However, we might not always be aware of how these impact our integration story. All Christians within a certain denomination and local church community operate with a key system of theological viewpoints, images, metaphors, categories, and themes (Stone & Duke, 2013).

While the contours of our faith have different emphases based on our own particular denominational affiliation, we also acknowledge that for many students it might not be possible to identify what is unique about their own church tradition until there is exposure to other church traditions and cultures. Additionally, one's own cultural and ethnic identity will also play a major role in how we inhabit the tradition of Christianity that we are familiar with. Some of the exercises at the end of our section will help you reflect on aspects of your own church culture. We hope you will then have dialogue with other students so that you can learn about some of these differences from your fellow students.

If you consider yourself nondenominational there are a couple of things to consider.[2] When we think of the word *denomination*, some may connect very quickly to this word, and some may not. Some who grew up in the church may have grown up in a distinct denomination, such as Baptist, Catholic, Episcopalian, Lutheran, Presbyterian, Pentecostal, Mennonite, or Methodist. However, many others may have grown up in a nondenominational/inter-denominational church, which became increasingly popular in the 1990s, all the way into the beginning of the 2000s.

Growing up, I (Carissa) went to a church that is best categorized as a Presbyterian church. Some of the unique aspects of this denomination were the use of printed liturgy, which is the order of worship for a church service (including Bible passages selected each week from the lectionary), the use of hymns as a part of corporate worship, and the regulated times when we stood up and sat down during the service. In high school, I joined a nondenominational church community that met in my school during weekdays, while still attending my home church on Sundays. This fellowship emphasized the unity of Christians across denominations. Needless to say, this experience was quite different. In this nondenominational church there were no hymns, people raised their hands during corporate singing, and the songs were sung in a more emotionally expressive manner (whether it be in joy or deep reflection).

---

[2]Nondenominational churches aren't really "nondenominational." They just don't openly proclaim a denomination, but if you look carefully, your pastor and church leaders all got their theological training somewhere and have certain theological influences. Consequently, these theological leanings have roots in certain denominations and are embedded in the theology that is taught and practiced at your church.

I really enjoyed the emphasis on interdenominational unity, and the experience was a breath of fresh air. Looking back, however, I realize we were not actually free of denominational influences or constraints, and in fact, no religious community could ever truly be nondenominational.

Even though this fellowship community did not claim to be of a particular denomination, we had influences from at least several denominations. Our time of singing was largely influenced by Pentecostal traditions, and our teaching was influenced by the Presbyterian tradition. The organizational structure in the leadership was largely influenced by collegiate Christian fellowships, such as InterVarsity. So, while we called ourselves nondenominational, we had distinct denominational influences in our community. In other words, there were specific ways in which we connected with God and one another in corporate worship that can be traced back to denominational influences and were very important to how we practiced our faith.

All of us engage in rituals as we connect with God and the church body, and these rituals are inevitably influenced by one or more denominational traditions. Over time, these rituals become a very special and sacred aspect of our spirituality. However, we may not realize all the ways that we are influenced by the ancient church and other denominational church traditions. We may not realize this because we often find ourselves surrounded by people who share in these rituals, and over time, we come to believe (implicitly or explicitly) that these rituals are simply "Christian." This is very similar to how culture is also often invisible to its own members. It's not until we encounter a church, community, or an individual with very different practices that we become aware of these differences. We realize that our church rituals are not simply "Christian," but believers engage with God and the body of Christ in many ways, and all are still considered Christian.

Reflective Exercise for Church Tradition

Up to this point in our integration story, we have been talking about Christian theology, which consists of two interrelated parts: the reading and interpretation of Scripture and church tradition. At this point, we'd like you to pause to reflect on both of these parts of the Christian theology storyline that compose integrative reflection. We'd like you to list ways you practice your faith that are deeply personal to you. We'd also like you to consider why it might be upsetting if these practices were taken away from you. We have listed a few prompts below that may help you get started.

1. What are certain passages of Scripture that are meaningful to you? Why are these particular passages meaningful? Does your own church community have passages of Scripture that are upheld as being important?

2. Is reading a Bible passage as a part of church service an important aspect of your Sunday ritual? If so, how are these passages selected?

3. How does your church community engage aspects of culture or race? What Scripture passages were important for your understanding of this?

4. Think about singing as a part of corporate worship. Is this important to you? What would it be like to not have singing as a part of church on Sundays? If singing is important, does your church primarily sing hymns, or is the music more contemporary?

5. What other aspects of corporate worship are important to you? How important is a time of confessional prayer? Is the Eucharist a part of weekly service? Should it be? Why or why not?

6. Some churches have prayer time at the conclusion of a church service, where congregants can go up and ask for prayers from prayer ministers. Is this an important part of your corporate worship time? Why or why not?

Reflecting on Scripture and church traditions and becoming more aware of these influences is one of the beautiful parts of coming to know our own integration story more. As we create space for denominational and local church traditions to be an active part of the integration conversation, we find that we bring a broader and more complex theology of God, human beings, sin, and human flourishing to the table. In cross-denominational dialogue, we also become aware of theological areas we previously had been unaware of.

Key Concept 2.3

Integration occurs when we thoughtfully reflect on our own interests and passions within the field of psychology and make connections with our Christian theology and culture storylines.

We now turn to discuss the psychology domain, the second part of the Integration Triad (see fig. 2.1). Since our readers are students of psychology, this domain is most likely the one that needs the least amount of introduction. As authors, we understand that psychological theory and research is a vital part of our integration storyline. In our first chapter we talked about how psychology is a collection of many different subdisciplines, many of which are very different from one another. (The APA recognizes fifty-four divisions, which are organizations that focus on various areas in psychology, including subdisciplines and topics of interest.) When we develop our own integrative views, we generally begin psychological reflection from the perspective of one or two of these psychological subdisciplines that we are more familiar with.

Surprisingly, out of all of the elements that we discuss in this book, psychology will be the one that gets the least amount of airtime. This is because we believe your other classes in your psychology major or graduate program have equipped you with a basic orientation to the science of human thought and behavior. In short, you have had (or will have) extensive training in how to think psychologically about a subject. Additionally, our main goal is to help you as students with the integration of disciplines by practicing interdisciplinary thinking and reflection between psychology and faith—not just to aid with thinking and writing within psychology alone.

We do, however, want to go a little more in-depth here on several points about psychology. First, when we speak about Christianity and our Christian faith, we discussed a history and tradition that has been developing for around two thousand years. In addition to this, we find that our beginning students in psychology are often surprised to hear us talk about psychology as a tradition with different movements, streams of thoughts and differing points of view. Psychology is a discipline that arose from its own historical context, being forged and hammered out in the furnace of the philosophy and scientific thinking of its own day.

It is true that some of the foundational thought of psychoanalytic psychology was based on naturalistic accounts of human personhood, and in the case of experimental psychology, its findings were (and still are) squarely based on the scientific method (Tyson et al., 2011; Whitney, 2020). That being said, psychology is not an objective discipline that is devoid of values, and theories within psychology often have an implicit philosophy about what it means to be human (Callaway & Whitney, 2022). Many times, the ethical component to psychological theory and practice directly overlaps with what Christians would believe, for example, working toward the healing and wholeness of human persons. At other times, there might be streams of psychological thought or theory that Christians might object to. For instance, some streams of psychology operate with a naturalistic philosophy that often reduces humanity to a series of behavioral or neurological processes. An example of this is Jesse Bering's (2012) work *The Belief Instinct*, which attempts to explain away the existence of God by reducing religion to an evolutionary byproduct of cognition that aided in survival. We recall here what we said earlier about narratives, and yes, even some streams of psychology have either explicit or implicit narratives.

That being said, there are still many points of overlap between psychology and the Christian faith, in addition to some points of disagreement. However, what we'd like you to understand is that when well-meaning Christians object to "psychology," they are mostly reacting to a version of psychology that they understand to be incompatible with their faith. They often do not understand that psychology has much more breadth and depth as a discipline. For instance, psychology is more than just a snapshot of what they might have heard about Freud. So, while not all aspects of psychology are in conflict with or stand as incompatible with the Christian faith, some presuppositions of psychological theory still need to be critically examined and reflected on.

Second, psychology already shapes and impacts the way that we read Scripture, whether we want to acknowledge this or not. As Joel Green (2008) notes, the question is not *if* science or psychology influences our reading of Scripture. Psychology and science *already do influence* our Christian faith, and the question we should ask is *which aspects* of psychology impact our reading of Scripture and *how* science or psychology already does influence our readings of Scripture (Green, 2008). Or to put it in a narrative framework: What narratives from psychology influence our reading and interpretations of Scripture? Another question worth considering for any student of psychology is how your reading of Scripture or certain aspects of your theology have changed or been informed since you have been studying psychology. Just as Christian theology can inform our faith, psychology can also influence or inform aspects of our Christian faith. By asking the question of how our reading of Scripture has been influenced by psychology, we are identifying some of the ways psychology has already informed or clarified our reading of Scripture.

Psychology is at its best when it clearly articulates observations about humanity's behavior and thought life that are measured, focused, tested, and repeatable through the use of experimentation. Remember that psychology provides a particular *type* of knowledge about human thought and behavior. From an integrative perspective, we have the opportunity to ask how this information from psychology helps inform or broaden our understanding of aspects of Christian theology or church practice.

Let's return for a moment to the story at the beginning of the chapter about the boy who had tried to die by suicide. The advice from his pastor was to "pray more" without helping him seek further professional therapy for suicidality. In this situation, the pastor held the theological belief that all mental health, even depression leading to suicidality, could be "cured" through a spiritual solution. The pastor might have also held beliefs that psychotherapy adopts views of the human person contrary to Christian thought and so cannot be trusted. The pastor might have also held certain theological beliefs that God only works in spiritual realms or in the church, but not outside of the church. All these theological assumptions taken together meant that this pastor held views that psychology could not inform or help shape his views on mental health. So, when we talk about psychology being an influence on our theology, much of how we allow our psychological beliefs to influence our theological ones is also determined by other theological inclinations or assumptions.

In Nicholas Wolterstorff's insightful book *Reason Within the Bounds of Religion*, Wolterstorff (1984) introduces the idea of control beliefs. Control beliefs are beliefs which help us sift and filter new information. Control beliefs help us understand what information aligns or is compatible enough with our other core beliefs. These control beliefs operate as a gatekeeper whereby we reject some new information and accept other pieces of information. Turning to the integration of theology and psychology, one's theological control beliefs shape the degree to which psychology informs or broadens[3] our theology. In the example given above, the pastor possibly held certain control beliefs that didn't allow psychology to shape the conversation or discourse at all. However, let's imagine that this same pastor held different control beliefs. Let's suppose this same pastor held theological control beliefs that God can work through counseling to bring about change. Let's also suppose that this pastor held beliefs that God's Spirit continues to work both inside and outside the church in both spiritual and relational realms to bring healing. If the pastor had held this set of control beliefs, then the outcome might be very different. This pastor would not have simply told the boy to "pray more." Instead, he most likely would have contacted other professional help. The only tricky thing about control beliefs is that they sometimes go unnoticed or unacknowledged. We should all do the work of examining our initial integrative ideas, which will also help us identify certain features of our theological control beliefs.

Wrapping Things Up

This chapter has painted a picture of integration consisting of three intersecting storylines that all intertwine and influence one another. We began by highlighting the importance of story and reflecting on the domains of Scripture, our own church tradition, aspects of our culture, and study and research within psychology. In this chapter, we are primarily focusing on the Christian theology and psychology storylines, while the next two chapters will be dedicated to exploring the culture storyline in more depth. Further

---

[3]The language of "informs" and "broadens" comes from Azusa Pacific University's faith development curriculum for faculty.

mindful reflection helps us develop our integrative viewpoints in a particular context within the field of psychology.

Understanding the different storylines of integration (Christian theology, psychology, and culture) will help you form your own ideas on integration. As long as we hold to our core Christian beliefs (such as those found in the ancient creeds), we can create space for slightly different versions or flavors of integration. This just means that we can welcome different perspectives of integration, since we will have different theological perspectives operating as control beliefs that allow us to interpret or adapt different aspects of psychological theory and research. Additionally, integration will look different between two people who have different cultural backgrounds and different interests in psychology. We believe that this diversity within the field of integration only enriches our collective work that we are each doing as we think about psychology and our Christian faith together.

Next, we touched briefly on how control beliefs often go unacknowledged. This underscores the importance of examining our initial integrative ideas by thinking about our Christian faith, and our passions and interests in psychology. One of the best ways to get familiar with our control beliefs is to examine what we are coming to the table with in regard to our church tradition, experiences, and culture. While we might not know all of the control beliefs we hold, the initial exercise of integration at least gets us in touch with some of the ideas we bring to the table, and then provides us an opportunity to develop these further on examination.

Consider here one of our students, Bethany Versoza, who used aspects of the Christian theology storyline and psychology storyline to reflect on her experience of having a brother with ASD

(Autism Spectrum Disorder).[4] She briefly describes how this experience impacted her views of psychology and her faith:

> Overall, in learning more in depth about ASD and the way it informs Christianity, I was again able to process emotions regarding this topic that hit so close to home. My experience with ASD is mostly based on familiarity with my brother, and impacted by psychological research that I have obtained throughout my undergraduate career. Reflections on our own stories of faith and psychology provided a space to zoom out and see the bigger picture on this personal topic . . . people with ASD must not be pushed to the side in regards to vocation and career interests; their families must be included and given tools that are needed to conquer the mountain ahead with support. . . . This culmination of my experience and research has allowed me to finalize what I truly believe. Picking my topic on ASD, in itself, was a healing process for me, especially considering that I am ending this class and my studies in psychology by combining my passion for my brother and those with disabilities, and my love for the Church and the Christian faith.

Bethany describes what it was like to learn more about her experience with her brother and how it informs her faith and psychology. It's a wonderful example of how we can begin to take our experience, and then reflect on that experience from the standpoint of our faith and psychology. We all have experiences in our lives that influence us, but often we don't have time to slow down and think how it might impact our lives and shape the way that we understand a topic in psychology or our faith. For Bethany, she had

---

[4]Used with permission.

lived with her brother much of her life, but when she was asked to reflect specifically on how her firsthand experience with ASD informed her Christian faith and her studies in psychology, she was able to come to a deeper understanding of autism and her faith. These moments and experiences of our own lives are all around us and part of our histories that make us who we are. But, just like Kierkegaard observes, it requires looking backwards in order for us to make meaning of these experiences and understand them. Bethany's story demonstrates how our work in psychology can be shaped by the Christian values of love of God, love of others, and justice that is restorative. It is to this framework of love and justice that we will now turn in our next chapter.

Reflection Questions

1. What are some ways that you have connected your faith with psychological topics you have learned about? List three to four psychological topics and the ways that they intersect with various elements of faith.

2. Using Bethany's story as a guide, and using the answers to the reflections on Christian theology above, how might your Christian theology inform or broaden how you think about an issue in psychology? List two to three ways that you can think of.

3. Think of a topic or subject within the discipline of psychology. How might this branch of psychology inform a subject or topic from Christian theology?

Love and Justice

A Theological Framework for Ethical Action and Cultural Awareness Within Integration

*The arc of the moral universe is
long, but it bends toward justice.*

THEODORE PARKER, POPULARIZED
BY MARTIN LUTHER KING JR.

*He has shown you, O mortal, what is good.
And what does the Lord require of you?
To act justly and to love mercy, and
to walk humbly with your God.*

MICAH 6:8

Have you ever been to or passed by a construction zone? A construction zone, whether it be a house, a high rise, or a freeway is typically very messy. My (Carissa's) dad is a retired architect and contractor, so growing up, I have many memories of visiting construction sites with him. They usually start with some degree of demolition which lasts for a period of time, depending on the project. While demolition occurs, the site would be perpetually messy for many months, where there are bricks, slippery ground and flooring, dark hallways without electricity, and large containers of liquid cement. After this demolition period, the construction would begin. Constructing a building is a meticulous process requiring much patience, care, and attention to detail. Although not linear by any means, the beginning of the process is often much messier than when the project is near completion. However, every construction project has one thing in common when it begins—all of them have plans of where the project is headed and what the final product will look like. Bags of sand, wood, steel, bricks, and liquid cement were more common at the beginning of a project. All of these materials are vital for laying the foundation and giving a framework for the structure. Toward the end, the structure of the building was more apparent, with flooring installed and buckets of paint half used. At the completion of the process, I would always be amazed at the beautiful, well-lit spaces and shiny tile floors, ready to serve their purpose. I often would find myself in awe that the dark mess I went to before is now a beautiful space.

These details about construction have a number of similarities to what can happen when we go through the process of reflecting on our faith, our interests in psychology, and our cultural background. First, as we have embarked on this integrative journey, we often see that integration is nonlinear, long, and sometimes messy, just like a construction project. As with any construction project, it takes time and patience for the entire project to be finished, and you can expect that it will be messy along the way. In fact, doing the work of integration often involves new or jarring experiences that force us to reexamine what we thought we already knew and cause us to reflect on our faith, psychology, and culture in new ways. Unlike a construction project, integration is a formative process that is never fully finished. Our Christian theology, our studies in psychology, and our culture inform how we practice integration, but these capacities continue to grow over time as we give them attention. Everyone's integration journey will be unique because of your own theological traditions and context, your cultural background, and the subdiscipline(s) of psychology that you are familiar with. While there's no single straightforward or linear path to practicing integration, there are some important guiding principles. This chapter on love and justice will highlight some of those principles from our Christian faith that are essential to the integration journey.

Second, in construction, no one begins a building project without knowing the direction or end goal of what they are doing. Can you imagine a contractor pouring a foundation and framing a building but not knowing the building's purpose or what the final product will be? Equally difficult is trying to build something without any plans for what the building will look like. With construction, the end goal of the building's purpose determines its overall design and all the smaller steps along the way. In a similar way, for the Christian practicing psychology we believe that the ultimate goal of our integration efforts is to join with the work of God to bring wholeness and healing in the particular context that you find yourself, by extending love and working for justice. It is this overall design and purpose for Christians practicing psychology that will guide our integrative journey, and the smaller steps along the way.

Here, we pick up and extend the themes we've introduced in our first chapter. Yes, integration occurs at the intersection of our

Christian faith, psychology, and our cultural/ethnic backgrounds as we thoughtfully reflect on each of these aspects. However, there is a further goal and purpose as Christians—which involves following Christ within a particular vocation within a particular context. Loving God and neighbor is an integral part of this work, and as we will see, from a Christian framework, this involves working toward restoration and justice within systems, people's lives, and communities. Just as my (Carissa's) dad would have a plan or blueprint for what a building would look like that would guide all of the smaller steps along the way, God's love for the world and movement of restorative justice through Jesus Christ provides the framework for our ethical action, research, and clinical practice within psychology.

This chapter is important in our integration journey, because integration isn't only about thinking or reflecting on the varied stories of our Christian theology, psychological interests, and culture. While this is an important starting point, our Christian faith also provides a goal or direction to shape us in our journey. That is, our Christian faith informs our work in psychology by providing Christians working within the field of psychology with a *telos* (i.e., a purpose or aim), which is new life or restoration and working toward greater love and justice in the particular context we find ourselves in (King & Whitney, 2015).

Working toward greater love and justice doesn't just happen. It requires us to be changed by God's Spirit as we grasp what God is up to in the world (Neff & McMinn, 2020). The integration of psychology and Christian theology can be presented as a topic to be thought about in a class, and we can learn different methods and models. However, it's a whole different thing as we let ourselves be changed by our integrative reflection, and we eventually develop new ways of thinking and behaving through reflection on our faith, psychology, and our cultural identity. In order to be truly loving in the way Jesus taught us, we not only have to call evil what it is, but we must also use our position to help advocate for the dignity of those who suffer or are on the margins of society. In order for Christians within the field of psychology to contribute to more just and equitable churches, families, and communities, their research and clinical practice needs to address injustices that occur on the individual, communal, societal, and global level (Callaway & Whitney, 2022; Dwiwardani & Whitney, 2022).

We're first going to dive a little deeper into this theological framework of love and justice for integration. In short, we believe that our Christian faith's emphasis on God's love for humanity through Jesus Christ moves us toward loving others and working toward justice in our own particular context. If you recall from our first chapter, integrative reflection between psychology and the Christian faith is never only an academic exercise, or something that can be reduced to the realm of thoughts or theories. It is embodied, lived, and has practical ramifications for our lives and the lives of others. Consequently, when viewed from the standpoint of our faith, the ultimate end of our work in psychology is joining with the work of God to bring wholeness and healing. In this chapter, we will examine more carefully how Scripture's narrative of creation, fall, redemption, and new creation shapes our integrative journey by providing a valuable framework for us to understand God's love and desire for justice. Next, we will discuss how love and justice are central and interrelated themes in Scripture that should inform our work we do in psychology as

Christians. Finally, we will look more closely at how the biblical themes of love and justice fit into the larger theme of God's restoration for the human creature, and clarify how this provides the impetus for the importance of addressing culture and diversity within the field of integration.

Key Concept 3.1

Love of God and love of neighbor are the end goal of integration.

For Christians, interpreting Scripture has always been central for our faith. Christians believe that God speaks to us through Scripture, and we rely on the Holy Spirit to direct and guide us as we read it. The Integration Triad (described in the previous chapters) is one of the ways we can begin shaping our integrative identity, but it is also part of our spiritual formation or growth, as we read Scripture, mindfully reflect on it, and listen to what God wants to say to us.

Reading and interpreting Scripture means more than simply "going back" and "retrieving" the ancient text in an objective way like a scientific observer (McKnight, 2018). Much of hermeneutical theory and biblical interpretation in the past has focused on historical criticism where the meaning of the biblical text was bound only to the historical situation and context of the author. Therefore, without the proper historical tools one was unable to be objective and discern meaning. In fact, in many approaches to biblical interpretation, the reader was thought of as someone who had to be distanced and neutral in order to discern the proper meaning (Murphy, 2018). Don't get us wrong; it is so important that we keep our wits about us and work to understand the background and details of the biblical story. We should learn all we can about the history, context, setting, and language of a particular text that we are reading. However, if we simply end it with historical investigation, then we have missed how Scripture has an ongoing, formative component for us as followers of Jesus (Green, 2008; Smith, 2009). We miss the vital question: What might God be saying to us through this biblical story or message? Here we return to our Augustinian principle of interpretation of Scripture that we discussed in chapter two. For Augustine, we must remember that the purpose of reading and interpreting Scripture is encountering God and God's love. Love of God and love for neighbor are the guiding principles as we read Scripture. Remember, Augustine's point was that many people can read Scripture, but the person who is actively loving God and loving neighbor will read Scripture differently than the one who is not. What difference does it make to be a Christian working within the field of psychology? From the ground that we have covered so far, we hope that you can see that our Christian faith and theology do matter for the work we do in psychology, since our work in psychology (or whatever we do) is informed by loving God and other people and by developing a greater capacity for working toward justice.

As we make connections between psychology and our cultural identities, we must remember that love of God and love of neighbor are central for the Christian. Loving God and others always involves an *encounter* with God. This is where we must return, and it also is where we also must begin. God's Spirit is working within the world to redeem, fashion, and form our lives. Situating integration within the context of encountering God, loving God, and loving neighbor means practicing reflection on faith, psychology, and culture that God can use to help draw us closer into a relationship with Christ.

Communities of Integration

To approach Scripture as an *encounter*, we are saying we hear, interact with, and relate to the God of the universe as we read Scripture. Or, as theologian John Webster (2003) puts it, Scripture has a unique place in divine revelation since it is the realm of encounter between the Holy Spirit, the human creature, and illumination of the divine knowledge of God. When we think of the work of integration from this perspective, we are acknowledging that as Christians we seek for the love and grace of Christ to shape us, and recognize that God's Spirit is actively forming and shaping us as we read Scripture.

When we think of *encounter*, we also cannot think that this means an encounter in an individualistic way, so that we somehow are encountering God apart from a community of faith. In fact, God is interested in shaping us into people who love and serve God (Green, 2008), and that formation best happens as we are in relationship with our communities of faith. Reading Scripture is best done in community with others, and we are shaped and formed as we do this. Additionally, communities that are invested in psychology and Christian theology are very important. Practicing integration means that we realize that God is shaping you and your peers in a particularly unique direction as you practice integration together. That is, God's Spirit is working among a group of you in a class or in a psychology department to shape and form you by God's love. When we think of it this way, this growth and development in love by God's Spirit is both exciting and humbling.

Key Concept 3.2

Creation, fall, redemption, and new creation provide the basic context to rightly understand God's love and justice.

We've discussed how the narrative of Scripture provides a framework for understanding our own lives, psychology, and cultural experiences. This naturally leads us to examine both love and justice from the perspective of four major themes within the narrative of Scripture: creation, fall, redemption, and new creation. Creation describes how God created the world good in the beginning and continues to sustain it; the fall describes how evil entered the world; redemption is the story of what God does about evil; and the theme of new creation discusses how God intends to make things right again in the future. Influenced by Reformed theologian Herman Bavinck (Wolters, 2005), the themes of creation, fall, redemption, and new creation provide a framework for understanding both love and justice for the integration of psychology and the Christian faith. Knowing that God's goal is to restore humanity and creation helps us understand that evil is ultimately overcome, and is the basis of Christian hope. This *telos* also provides us with a way to understand injustice, suffering, and brokenness in this world. We find within Christian Scripture that there are graphic descriptions of pain, suffering, and injustice since we live in a world where sin has entered the picture. However, Christianity does not overlook the presence of evil or injustice. It does not try to gloss over the reality of evil. In fact, Christianity calls evil what it is, and does not downplay or diminish how evil breaks the bonds of relationship and love that God intended to govern and permeate human existence.

Creation. We begin with a trinitarian account of creation—how God exists eternally in relationship as Father, Son, and Spirit and creates the world out of love. While Genesis is the chief passage to describe the creation of the world in the beginning, the themes of creation are also found throughout Scripture. God continues to uphold and sustain creation over time through the Spirit (Job 34:14-15), and redeems the world through the Son, Jesus Christ (John 3:16).

First, adopting a trinitarian understanding of creation and human personhood helps us understand the social and relational aspects of humanity (Gunton, 2005). This is because the doctrine of the Trinity (God existing as Father, Son, and Spirit) expresses an important ontology or reality about God's being—that God exists fundamentally in relationship (Gunton, 2003). Because God exists as Father, Son, and Spirit, this relational component is also found within the created order. God's relationality establishes the relational and personal aspects of humanity that are so central to what we study in the discipline of psychology (Gunton, 2003). Moreover, a trinitarian account of creation and persons helps to move us away from dualistic approaches of personhood that separate mind from body. In short, a trinitarian conception of creation helps us firmly root the relational and embodied components of human nature in a solid theological foundation.

Second, the goodness of creation (Genesis 1) sets a standard for the order of the universe, and how humans exist in relationship with God, others, their own selves, nonhuman creatures, and the earth (Callaway & Whitney, 2022). According to Scripture, these relationships that God created in the beginning existed in a state of shalom, which describes a wholeness and abundance to life. Creation (before sin entered the world) is important to understand, since it provides a baseline for how things were intended to be and how to understand what went wrong. To understand something as fallen or broken implies the existence of a proper order, or how things *should* be (Lewis, 2012).

Third, there is an ongoing goodness that can still be found in creation. Known as common grace (Kuyper, 1961), this is God's grace that is bestowed to believers and nonbelievers alike (Whitney, 2020; King & Whitney, 2015). It is rooted in the idea that God's goodness is freely given to all, as seen in Matthew 5:45, where God "causes his sun to rise on the evil and the good, and sends rain on the righteous and the unrighteous." Common grace provides a foundation for Christians to engage with the created order, discover truths within creation, and learn from other humans, including non-Christians. It is also the basis of how we can discern truths about the world through disciplines like science or psychology. King and Whitney (2015) argue that because believers and nonbelievers are all created in the image of God (by his grace), all humans have the capacity to thrive and grow, whether or not they are intentional about this. As such, Christians need not limit themselves to studying psychological theories and literature only produced by other Christians. Through common grace, non-Christians can still discover truths about the natural world and humanity. This doesn't mean that we don't need to be discerning about what we study, read, or learn; it just means that there's much truth and wisdom available about humans and human nature since God allows truths about the natural world to be disclosed to those who inquire (Whitney, 2020).

Fourth, a trinitarian account of creation establishes relationality as central to human life. Humans stand in relation to God, others, and our own selves, *and* we also stand in relation to the earth. As stewards over creation who relate to the earth (not to dominate it), we are given the responsibility to tend, care, and develop the context we inhabit (Whitney, 2020). God graciously allows humans to shape and fashion the world where we live. For instance, this shaping and fashioning could look like planting a garden where there was not one before, or shaping the world through research or clinical practice in psychology.

Fall. As mentioned earlier, the message of Christianity does not overlook pain and suffering that is caused by sin, or how humans or the rest of the created order is hurt because of it. We as humans *are* hurt by sin. We live as people who sin (we go against God's good design for living), but we have also been sinned against (people hurt us either intentionally or unintentionally because they too have gone against God's good design for living well). Thus, we commit sin as individuals, but we also stand in a line of people who have sinned before us. These collective sins spread out like ripples in water, impacting our thought patterns and the ways that we relate to others. The more that we move through this life, the more we understand and see that hate brings about more hate. I (William) remember hearing a shocking and angering news story of two parents who abused their elementary-age daughter by locking her in a closet for much of the day and night when she wasn't in school. When social workers finally found her, she was scared and malnourished. Her rescuers asked her why she had never said anything to her teachers, and she responded that she just thought that all parents locked their children in closets. Her parents' sinful acts of neglect created ripple effects where this kind of extreme abuse and neglect was the only reality that this young girl knew. She had just assumed that all children encountered this same reality of being locked in closets. The parents' abuse and sinful actions will continue to have ripple effects that will impact their daughter's social, emotional, and cognitive growth. Injustice and racial violence are other examples of the ripple effects of sin. While individual acts of injustice and racism are clearly sinful, individual acts are motivated by ideologies and implicit biases that stretch beyond a particular individual. Individuals are shaped in contexts and environments that foster or promote racist or unjust ideas (Romero & Liou, 2023). The contexts and environments that breed hate and injustice represent the systemic nature of sin (as well as the systemic nature of racism; Beed & Beed, 2015).

God's intention is to have people live in harmony and shalom, in a right relationship with God, self, others, nonhuman creatures, and the earth. Even though sin entered the world, God still desires that the human creature and created world thrive and flourish. Although sin disrupted what God created in the beginning, God made (and still makes) provisions so that humans can ensure the fullest life possible.

For instance, one of these initial provisions for Israel to live life well is found in the Torah and the Ten Commandments. For Israel, these were divine blueprints for living life well. While many people who are not Jewish or Christian might dismiss the idea of the Ten Commandments being applicable to modern-day life, consider for a moment if just for a day, everyone in the world agreed to follow these ten rules for living (Plantinga, 2002). For one day, no one would be murdered. For one day, no one would lie or cheat. No one would steal. No one would get mugged and robbed of their money. People would honor the relationships that they have committed themselves to. People would have a respect for one another, and not be driven by jealousy or greed. People would have a degree of respect for their parents, partners, and children. Wars and civil unrest that are driven by greed and lust for more land, money, or power would cease for a day.

Having a break from violence, strife, envy, greed, and murder (for even a day) begins to sound pretty good when we think about it this way. We don't know many folks who would say that an end to violence and hate would not be a good thing—even if it was for a day. When we think about it, we begin to see that God has given us guidance on how to live well; however, individuals, communities, and systems of power continually fail to live up to how God wants us to live. These are the unfortunate results of the fall. Genesis tells of Adam and Eve committing the first sin, but we all follow their pattern. Unfortunately, we stand within a culture or system that often makes it difficult to live in God's love and treat others how we would want to be treated. When sin entered the world, the fall brought with it ripple effects that fundamentally changed the fabric of the created realm (in both the human and nonhuman creation; Whitney, 2020). This change impacted all domains of life: biological, psychological, social, and spiritual. With the entrance of sin in the world comes all kinds of disruption of human relationship, and things are never as they should be with sin (Plantinga, 2002).

Redemption. While Christianity has much to say about sin and the fall of humanity, God does not leave humanity or the rest of creation on our own path toward destruction. Redemption through Jesus Christ is central to the message of Christianity, and God is in a continual process of restoring all of creation and setting things right. In Scripture, God's story of redemption is displayed through the nation of Israel, their eventual freedom from Egypt, the establishment of their own land, and God's acts of love culminating through the person and work of Jesus to save and redeem humanity. In fact, the redemption (or salvation event) of the Old Testament is rescuing the Israelites from slavery in Egypt. However, throughout the Old and New Testament, it is very clear that redemption involves not only individual salvation, but also the restoration of both individuals and societies from brokenness (Brueggemann, 1995).

Redemption hinges on Jesus Christ, since through Christ all of the promises of God throughout Scripture are brought to completion. Jesus lives a sinless life. He suffers and dies for the sins of humanity because of God's great love for the world. But he also does something that humans could never do—Jesus ultimately overcomes evil and death through his resurrection from the dead. God's gift of saving humanity through Jesus is what God's grace is all about. It is undeserved and something that transforms the person who receives the gift. Redemption through Jesus Christ is God's way of restoring humanity and the rest of creation to God's original design before the fall (Wolters, 2005). With Jesus, God's kingdom breaks into our reality in a new way; however, we still wait for the final days when evil will be eradicated completely.

The doctrine of redemption provides a foundation for us in the psychology profession to engage in the difficult work of facing human brokenness on a daily basis. In the story of redemption, we partner with God in the ongoing work of "doing good" (Galatians 6:9), working within our discipline of psychology to help restore human functioning and relationships. Furthermore, we are called to work toward the restoration of broken systems and structures that hurt and oppress humanity. The biblical story of redemption sets a precedent for psychology students and professionals to actively work toward shalom by restoring systems and structures (Entwistle, 2015; King & Whitney, 2015). As Christians within psychology in our work of psychotherapy or psychological research, we can join with the work of God in redeeming patterns of human behavior by helping people understand how they relate to themselves, others, and the world around them (Whitney, 2020).

New creation/restoration. The work of redemption has begun, but the created world is not yet how it should be. Ultimately, God's work of redemption and restoration will culminate when Jesus returns the second time, known as the consummation of the ages (Entwistle, 2015). In theological terms, the study of what will happen at the end of time is called *eschatology*. One day, God will bring restoration in a new heaven and new earth (Revelation 21:1-2). In the end, God will restore humans' relationships with nature, each other, and God. This is the essence of what Revelation 21:5 depicts when God says, "I am making everything new!" Until that time though, we as Christians join with the work of God as God's love breaks into the present and provides glimpses of hope, love, justice, and peace. On an integrative note, when a psychologist or therapist works to help restore relationships through counseling or psychotherapy, for example, she is involved in God's work of restoration by restoring humans' connections with one another. Thus, work done as a psychologist or in psychology is part of our vocation as we join with the ongoing work that God is doing in the world while we await the ultimate restoration accomplished when God renews all things (Entwistle, 2015; Wright, 2006). This means that Christians who work within psychology have a part to play in extending God's love and working for justice. This oftentimes manifests itself in restoring broken relationships through psychotherapy or addressing injustices through psychological research. As Christians who are also psychologists, we understand that God desires life for his creation, and this involves the prospering and flourishing of human life—which also means addressing injustices that inhibit God's creation from becoming what it was truly meant to be.

In sum, the narrative of creation, fall, redemption, and new creation provides a framework for understanding how the world was created, why evil still exists, and how Christ has restored and is restoring humanity and the rest of the created order. As humans created in the image of God, we also can join with God in this plan of restoration by working toward some aspects of restoration in the context where we have been placed. We say "some aspects" of restoration because there are some things that only the Holy Spirit can do (such as bring others to salvation). However, we can work to extend God's love to others and be open to what God's Spirit can do through our actions in the particular place where we live and work.

Our source of Christian hope is knowing that God will redeem and restore the earth, as well as eradicate evil and bring about justice. Until that time, we live knowing that ultimate restoration will come, but it has not occurred yet. Christian theologians have often called this the already/not yet aspect of the kingdom of God. In short, hope and healing came into the world in a new way through Jesus. God's kingdom is "already" established through Jesus' earthly ministry, death, and resurrection; however, God's kingdom is still "not yet" fully realized by everyone. We wait until the final return of God to restore all things and make them new. In this period of waiting for the final return of Christ, restoration continues to occur in human lives and relationships through God's grace and provision, whether humans acknowledge God's gracious, loving action or not. When viewed from a theological perspective, the ultimate end of psychological science (and our work within psychology) is joining with the work of God to bring wholeness and healing by working toward love and justice in the context and community that we have been placed in (Callaway & Whitney, 2022). It is to a more extensive discussion of love and justice that we now turn.

Key Concept 3.3

Love, justice, and shalom are interconnected realities that God desires for humanity.

Encounters with God's love. In Callaway and Whitney's (2022) book *Theology for Psychology and Counseling*, five Christian themes are identified that serve as an ethical guide for Christians practicing psychology. These five Christian themes are justice, love, hope, grace, and hospitality. While all of these Christian themes overlap with work that is done within psychology, we will elaborate more on the Christian conceptions of love and justice here, since we have described how the process of integration moves us to extend love and to work toward greater justice in our own particular context. From the perspective of our Christian faith, justice and love always go together. Since God is lovingly committed to creation (i.e., to humanity and the rest of the world), God is also against injustices that destroy both human and nonhuman creation (animals, plants, trees, etc.).

The message of Scripture is that God creates the world (and humanity) out of love. God freely creates because love seeks to share its goodness (Barth, 1961). Theologian Stanley Grenz (2000) notes that "the act of creation is the outflowing of the eternal love relationship with the triune God" (p. 101). Because of God's great love, God continues to care and sustain the human creature, even if humanity does not respond to God's love (Kuyper, 1961). God's love is vast and deep and wide. One of the frequent descriptions of God's love in the Old Testament is that it is steadfast, everlasting, and abundant—communicated by the Hebrew word *hesed*. In short, God's love is characterized by a wholehearted commitment to the human creature (e.g., Psalms 86:15; 136:26; Jeremiah 31:3); it does not stop and cannot be used up. God's love consistently shows up to uphold, protect, and restore the world and the human creature. To put it another way, God's love toward humanity and creation is so committed, so fierce, and so strong that "sin has no power to break God's faithfulness to God's own original intentions," as theologian Kathryn Tanner skillfully puts it (Tanner, 2010a).

In the New Testament, we find that first and foremost, God is love (1 John 4:8) and God loved the world so much that he sent Jesus (John 3:16). Jesus is the ultimate expression and embodiment of God's love. Moreover, God's love expressed through Christ becomes the foundation for humans acting in loving ways. The apostle Paul makes the connection between deeply understanding the vast nature of God's love and this understanding changing and strengthening us. In Ephesians 3:17-19, he prays that the church in Ephesus, "being rooted and established in love, may have power, together with all the Lord's holy people, to grasp how *wide and long and high and deep is the love of Christ,* and to know this love that surpasses knowledge" (emphasis added). In another letter, when Paul writes to the church in Corinth (1 Corinthians 13:13), he waxes eloquent about the importance of how humans should do all things with love, and calls love the "greatest" of Christian virtues, rising even above both faith and hope (Callaway & Whitney, 2022).

Turning to the intersection of love and cultural identity, God's love extends to all of humanity, regardless of race, class, gender, sexual orientation, or economic status. God's love knows no boundaries, as theologian Miroslav Volf reminds us, and humans do not need to be innocent of wrongdoing in order to be loved by God or by the church (Volf, 2019). The commandment to love our neighbor as ourselves (Matthew 22:37-39; Mark 12:30-31) does not simply mean to extend love only to those who are similar to us. Extending neighborly love includes extending love to those who are different from us, and especially those who are on the margins of society and different from us ethnically. In the parable of the good Samaritan (Luke 10:25-37), Jesus specifically picked a Jew and a Samaritan (representing different ethnic groups) because Jews and Samaritans hated each other. It is not incidental that Jesus chose these ethnic backgrounds in the parable of the good Samaritan to highlight who our neighbor really is (Hays, 2008; Whitney et al., 2023). As the apostle John exhorts, it is impossible to say that we love God and yet hate our brother or sister (1 John 4:19-21).

As we will elaborate further in chapter four, Jesus' Jewishness located him within a particular ethnic identity. Here we must remember that ethnic diversity is present within Scripture and that God is the Creator of diversity. We find that there is a great diversity of people and people groups represented within the Bible. Scripture speaks of people from different nations (Hebrew: *goy*; Greek: *ethnos*), and yet, it does not advocate for racial superiority or racial inferiority (Whitney et al., 2023). In God's kingdom, God-given diversity is not a reason for division, oppression, or hate (Deddo, 1997) since all humans are created in the image of God (Genesis 1:27-28). In fact, throughout Scripture, the worth and value of human lives are stressed—those of women, men, and children, those with different abilities (John 9:1-3), and those from all nations and cultures (1 Kings 8:41-43). God's love for all humanity becomes the basis for our affirming the full dignity and respect of every person (Whitney et al., 2023).

Jesus' message and ministry reached across the cultural and ethnic divisions of the day, highlighting that even those outside Israel were not outside the bounds of God's love (Whitney et al., 2023). Humans are social and relational creatures, since we have been created by the God of relationship—and the foundation of this relationship is ultimately one of love (Grenz, 2000). In fact, both psychology and Christian theology are in agreement that one primary aspect of being a human is that we exist in relationship with other human beings. If God is love and acts consistently out of love, then it makes sense that humans should also relate to one another out of love. One of the most poignant portraits of unity, diversity, love, and restoration occurs in the final book of the Bible. Revelation 7 depicts a great multitude from every tribe, tongue, and nation worshiping the Lamb. The picture is a vivid one, with humanity (being represented with all of their differences in ethnicity and language) uniting as one in worship of the Creator (Callaway & Whitney, 2022). It is clear that even in the end of time, ethnic divisions are not obliterated or homogenized in this picture of worship. God, through Jesus Christ, is in the business of sustaining and redeeming all of humanity and bringing wholeness to human lives.

Encounters with God's justice. Any talk about justice from a Christian perspective must have the love of God as the backdrop, and no discussion about justice can be separated from the embodiment of God's love found in Jesus Christ. Just as the love of God is the central theme throughout the narrative of Scripture (expressed in the Old Testament as God's covenant with Israel, and in the New Testament through the person and work of Jesus Christ), justice is the active part of God's commitment to uphold the human creature and God's creation. On the other hand, because of sin humanity has a proclivity and propensity to destroy that which God has created. God consistently stands against those things that destroy humanity, but he also desires for the human community to be an example of God's mercy and love to others (Callaway & Whitney, 2022).

As biblical scholars have noted, there are two Hebrew words that Old Testament writers commonly use to describe the idea of justice: *mishpat* and *tsedaqah*. These words often occur as a pair in the Old Testament and are commonly translated as "justice" (*mishpat*) and "righteousness" (*tsedaqah*; Brueggemann, 1995; Callaway & Whitney, 2022). While our English words *justice* and *righteousness* begin to put us on the right track of how we might understand these Hebrew words, the actual meanings of these words carry a depth that often gets overlooked when they are translated to English.

First, when the Old Testament speaks of justice, justice is never doled out in an arbitrary manner by God, but is necessary because of God's faithfulness to sustain the community of Israel. In fact, *tsedaqah* carries the notion of rule that is characterized by faithfulness—implying a strong relational component to the word (Goldingay, 2019). Similarly, *mishpat* can be translated as justice or authority with the idea that justice needs to be administered so as to promote equity and harmony within one's community (Mafico, 1992). God creates the world, establishing equity and justice (Psalm 99:4), and continues to be the righteous judge (Psalm 7:11) who expects Israel to be a community that exemplifies God's justice (Deuteronomy 1:16-17) where people treat each other with dignity, equity, and fairness (Mafico, 1992). Thus, when the terms *justice* (*mishpat*) and *righteousness* (*tsedaqah*) are used together, these richly relational words remind us that God cares about the way that we treat other people within our communities. Justice is one of the ways that we ensure that people and their communities flourish. According to Old Testament scholar and theologian Walter Brueggemann (1986), when the prophets called for justice and righteousness, they were referring to an order in human society that is viable and sustainable—one in which neighbors can dwell in solidarity with one another. Consequently, God's call for justice was necessary when Israel neglected ethical commitments and people were overlooked, marginalized, taken advantage of, silenced, or oppressed (Brueggemann, 2016). In fact, God is particularly angry when rulers, or people in authority, who are supposed to be committed to upholding the flourishing of community, use their power to oppress and pervert justice. Take Micah 3:9-11 as an example:

> Hear this, you leaders of Jacob,
>> you rulers of Israel,
> who despise justice (*mishpat*)
>> and distort all that is right;
> who build Zion with bloodshed,
>> and Jerusalem with wickedness.
> Her leaders judge for a bribe,
>> her priests teach for a price,
>> and her prophets tell fortunes for money.
> Yet they look for the LORD's support and say,
>> "Is not the LORD among us?
>> No disaster will come upon us."

Here, Micah speaks out against rulers and authorities who have used their power to seek material prosperity and comfort at the expense of those they were supposed to protect. Justice (*mishpat*) is despised and distorted because these leaders have not been equitable and fair, and they arrogantly think that God will protect them because they are in positions of authority. Consequently, the normal bonds of human relationship that God wants for humanity are broken and distorted. Yes, we individually have obligations to each other to be fair, kind, and generous, but in addition to this, people who have power also have the responsibility to see that their communities act with fairness, kindness, and generosity (Goldingay, 2019).

Second, we've discussed how when humans are called to exhibit justice and righteousness, the emphasis is on right relations between humans. We've also seen that the life of every human is of value to God (since all humans are created in God's image). As a result, God is particularly angry when people are marginalized and oppressed because it represents a violation of justice, faithfulness, and love. Texts such as Jeremiah 22:3 make the connection between justice, righteousness, and rescuing those who are oppressed and marginalized: "Do what is just (*mishpat*) and right (*tsedaqah*). Rescue from the hand of the oppressor the one who has been robbed. Do no wrong or violence to the foreigner, the fatherless or the widow, and do not shed innocent blood in this place."

Here, the foreigner, the fatherless (orphans), and widows are particular groups mentioned because they had a history of being oppressed, marginalized, and neglected within the community of Israel in Jeremiah's day. God is not just interested in their survival, but is *especially* concerned for their well-being. Notice how justice and righteousness are connected with specific action, which involves not only refraining from hurting or doing wrong, but also rescuing those who have been wronged. In short, when justice and righteousness are administered according to God's standards, it involves action.

When we speak of God's justice here on earth, human agency is always involved since God's desire is for humans to live out and practice justice within their social groups and the wider society. However, it is not good enough to simply agree that justice would be a good thing (or that the idea of justice is something to work toward in the future). Justice always involves action because the way we live out our lives is through human relationships. In short, God is concerned with how we treat one another through our actions. Israel is supposed to be concerned for the marginalized because they know what it was like to be enslaved and be foreigners in the land of Egypt. Thus, Exodus 23:9 commands: "Do not oppress a foreigner; you yourselves know how it feels to be foreigners, because you were foreigners in Egypt." God expects Israel to show others mercy, justice, and love, because God was merciful and heard their cries when the Israelites were enslaved. Moreover, the connection between love and justice is also found in the prophetic literature of the Hebrew Bible. For instance, in Zechariah 7:9-10 God commands Israel to "Administer true justice (*mishpat*); show mercy and compassion to one another. Do not oppress the widow or the fatherless, the foreigner or the poor. Do not plot evil against each other."

The groups mentioned in Jeremiah and Zechariah as marginalized or oppressed are just a representation of folks who were oppressed in biblical times. While these same groups are still marginalized today (widows, orphans, immigrants, the poor), this text does not exclude us from interpreting it in light of other groups that are victims of oppression, hate, and cruelty in contemporary times. We have to understand that women, BIPOC, LGBTQIA individuals, and many other groups have experienced oppression and marginalization more than other groups. In this way, we must read these passages about justice in the Old Testament with an eye toward greater action to work with those who have been historically marginalized (Hook et al., 2023). Justice flows from God's love and desire for righteousness. In fact, anything that threatens the survival, security, and flourishing of marginalized groups is an issue of the sacredness of life, as ethicist David Gushee (2013) rightly notes. Justice is a commitment to right relations between people, and part of our role as Christians is to rightly identify those who are vulnerable and work toward establishing right relations with those who have been marginalized (Gushee, 2013).

Third, we cannot miss the important fact that the overarching theme of justice is connected with restoration and shalom within Scripture. Features of shalom are available in the present, while the full redemption and restoration of humanity and creation is yet to occur. Recall how we previously discussed the new creation (within the themes of creation, fall, redemption, and new creation) and how God is working to restore and renew all of creation. God's justice *is* restorative justice, as Chris Marshall correctly points out. Justice is satisfied when there is peace and restoration within relationships, and not simply punishment for wrongdoing (Marshall, 2012). This biblical vision of restorative justice also goes against what many in our society might think of when they hear the word *justice*. For instance, many think of justice entailing retribution, or retributive justice, which is the idea that justice is about people being punished when they do wrong, and that wrongdoers need to pay for what they have done (Marshall et al., 2018). While we do find cases in Scripture that seem to be retributive in nature, there is a strong case to be made that on a *macro* level, the message of Scripture is one large movement of God's love and restorative justice working to redeem humanity and the rest of creation (Gunton, 2003; Marshall, 2012). For instance, renowned New Testament scholar N. T. Wright describes justice as the "intention of God, expressed from Genesis to Revelation, to set the whole world right" (Wright, 2008). Consequently, we find in Scripture that justice and righteousness result in peace and restoration—which is where the concept of restorative justice comes from. Chris Marshall (2012) notes that this is seen within the books of Isaiah and the Psalms. Take Isaiah 32:16-17, for example.

> The LORD's justice (*mishpat*) will dwell in the desert,
>> his righteousness (*tsedaqah*) live in the fertile field.
> The fruit of that righteousness (*tsedaqah*) will be peace (*shalom*);
>> its effect will be quietness and confidence forever.

Here we see again that *mishpat* and *tsedaqah* are used together. However, we also see the results of the relational and action-oriented components of justice and righteousness being carried out. That is, when God's justice and righteousness are firmly established, peace (*shalom*) will occur and be established in the land (Marshall, 2012). If we only think of justice in a punitive way, this verse doesn't quite make sense; quietness and confidence are not always the natural results of someone getting punished. However, when we understand justice as a type of faithfulness that moves to restore relationships and communities, then it makes sense that wholeness, well-being, quietness, and confidence are the results. It becomes quite clear that human flourishing or thriving cannot happen without God's restorative justice. Thus, justice (in the biblical sense) is not simply punishment; it also implies the restoration of a situation or environment that promotes equity and harmony in a community (Mafico, 1992).

Another example of this is found in Psalm 72:1-4.

> Endow the king with your justice (*mishpat*), O God,
>> the royal son with your righteousness (*tsedaqah*).
> May he judge your people in righteousness (*tsedaqah*),
>> your afflicted ones with justice (*mishpat*).

> May the mountains bring prosperity (*shalom*) to the people,
>> the hills the fruit of righteousness (*tsedaqah*).
> May he defend the afflicted among the people
>> and save the children of the needy;
>> may he crush the oppressor.

This psalm represents a prayer for the king of Israel. Again, the fruit of proper justice and righteousness is shalom for the people. While the NIV translates *shalom* as "prosperity," we could also translate *shalom* as "wholeness" (well-being or peace) since all these words together give us a more complete picture of shalom.

We also see here how justice involves action. In fact, prosperity occurs when those in authority rule ethically, defending the cause of those who are afflicted, needy, or oppressed. The psalm longs for the kind of righteous rule that enables peace and prosperity to last forever. Another compelling part of this particular psalm is how it goes on to describe how other nations (outside Israel) will also be blessed by this administration of justice. Old Testament scholar and professor John Goldingay notes that the connection between justice, faithfulness, and prosperity (*shalom*) functions both as a "prayer and challenge" to those who were ruling Israel (Goldingay, 2019). In fact, faithfulness to one's community through justice is the key to well-being in every part of the life of the community (Goldingay, 2019). Said another way, when there are injustices in our communities and societies, everyone suffers, not only those who are oppressed. In God's vision of justice both the oppressor and oppressed need transformation. The oppressor needs to be transformed so that they might use their authority to establish loving and ethical rules that promote well-being for the entire community, while the oppressed and marginalized need to be transformed by being restored to wholeness and well-being. God's desire is for each and every person to experience shalom, however, this is impossible if the groans and cries of the suffering or victimized are not listened to (Gushee, 2013). God's restorative justice seeks to bring people into renewed relationship with God and with each other, to restore people to wholeness, and enable the human community to find well-being. In Scripture, it is clear that God stands on the side of those who are marginalized, and he calls us to dismantle unjust systems that cause oppression and injustice. God assures us that justice will be administered in the end of time when all humanity stands before God; however, we live in the current time when the church of Christ is expected to be an example of the faithful love and justice of God (Callaway & Whitney, 2022).

Fourth, if God's desire is for people to rule with justice and faithfulness, then it makes sense that Jesus, who brings about God's kingdom in a new way here on earth, would be God's ambassador who also upholds justice, peace, and restoration (McConnell et al., 2021a).[1] In the New Testament, God's love and justice are embodied in Jesus Christ. When Jesus proclaims God's kingdom, he is speaking of the rule of God being established on the earth through his own ministry, and ultimately through his death and resurrection. We see Jesus doing that which Israel and Israel's leaders could not always do: standing with those who are marginalized, administering restorative justice, and breaking social norms

---

[1]McConnell et al., (2021a) have correctly drawn attention to the connection between diversity, justice, and peace, and we have appreciated their contributions to this subject. See further McConnell, J. M., Bacote, V., Davis, E. B., Brown, E. M., Fort, C. J., Liu, T., Worthington, E. L., Hook, J. N., & Davis, D. E. (2021). Including multiculturalism, social justice and peace within the integration of psychology and theology: Barriers and a call to action. *Journal of Psychology and Theology, 49*(1), 5–21.

whenever they went against the love of God or love of neighbor (e.g., Jesus overturning the temples' money changers or his healing on the Sabbath). Jesus dines with "sinners" and welcomes those who are outcast by society for whatever reason. By going against the social norms of his day, Jesus demonstrates what God's love and justice actually look like. In fact, when Jesus instructed his followers to put God's kingdom and righteousness first (as in Matthew 6:33), to Jesus' Jewish audience, this was another way of saying to make *tsedaqah* and *mishpat* a priority in their lives (Goldingay, 2019). Another example is found in Luke 4:18-19, where the prophetic vision of justice and Jesus' ministry are seen as intertwined. In this chapter, Jesus is just beginning his earthly ministry after being tempted in the desert. He enters into the synagogue in Nazareth and is given a portion of Scripture from Isaiah to read. He proclaims:

> The Spirit of the Lord is on me,
> > because he has anointed me
> > to proclaim good news to the poor.
> He has sent me to proclaim freedom for the prisoners
> > and recovery of sight for the blind,
> to set the oppressed free,
> > to proclaim the year of the Lord's favor. (Luke 4:18-19)

When Jesus announces that this Scripture has now been fulfilled, he is indicating that he is the one that brings justice by healing, proclaiming freedom for those imprisoned, and offering freedom to those who are oppressed (Callaway & Whitney, 2022). Jesus is in the business of administering justice and bringing restoration that fulfills the kind of faithful rule that the prophets were calling for in the Old Testament. As Joel Green (1997) notes, Jesus refuses to accept the socially determined boundaries of his time, by declaring that even those who were perceived as outsiders are deserving of God's grace. As seen in the Old Testament with justice, the good news of Jesus' ministry always involved action—it was something practical, lived, and felt. Thus, God's kingdom is a new reality that is tangible and real—embodied in a new way in Jesus Christ, and embodied by Christ's followers that are anointed by the Spirit (Acts 2:1-21). This is also why the apostle Paul describes the gospel as the "righteousness" of God that has been revealed or made known in Jesus—since Jesus is the embodiment of God's love and justice (Romans 3:21-22; Marshall, 2012). Thus, Jesus' life, ministry, death, and resurrection operate as the new frame of reference for both God's love and restorative justice found within the New Testament (Marshall, 2012).

Wrapping Things Up

We began this chapter discussing how love and justice from a Christian perspective provide a theological framework for ethical action and cultural awareness. The commandments to love our neighbor as ourselves (Matthew 22:37-39) and to act justly (Micah 6:8) are not simply things that God is asking us to think about. They are Christian theological concepts rooted in God's gracious actions that require us, as humans, to act, and to pursue right and faithful love toward our neighbors. As we saw in the case of the good Samaritan, loving our neighbor is not simply loving our friends and relatives, but loving those who might be different from us—especially those who are suffering or oppressed.

In fact, Christians should use the platform that they have been given to work toward both love and justice in their particular area of psychology where they have been called. However, in order for Christians within the field of psychology to extend their work toward justice, their research and clinical practice need to address injustices that occur on the individual, communal, societal, and global level. Consequently, issues of culture and diversity are essential to address within the integration dialogue because, from a Christian framework, becoming aware and understanding another's cultural background is a way to rightly love our neighbor. As we have seen in this chapter, one's ethnicity is something that is created by God, and since we have all been made in God's image, we are called to extend love and to work toward justice—regardless of people's ethnic or cultural background. In our next chapter we will expand more on owning our cultural background and understanding the cultural background of others as an exercise of both love and justice. Knowing that God desires love and justice to be extended to those who are marginalized or oppressed gives us a vision of why these things matter in the integration dialogue between our Christian faith and psychology. Shaped by this vision of love and justice, we now have a practical plan and framework to move forward and think about how Christians can be part of the solution for bringing hope, healing, and restoration to the particular context where we research or practice psychology.

Reflection Questions

1. Were you familiar with the themes of creation, fall, redemption, and new creation? If not, was this framework helpful? Why or why not?

2. What were your views about love and justice before you read this chapter? How have your views changed after reading this chapter?

3. According to the authors, how are love and justice a framework for cultural awareness and ethical action?

4. What is the concept of restorative justice about? How might you envision your work within psychology to be shaped in a way that moves toward restorative justice?

Integration Is Culturally Embedded

*What you see and what you hear depends
a great deal on where you are standing.*

C. S. Lewis, *The Magician's Nephew*

We are now moving to an essential topic within the interdisciplinary dialogue of Christian faith and psychology that hasn't been emphasized as much in the history of integration (Shelton & Dwiwardani, 2022). Because of this, we will expand on the cultural aspects of the Integration Triad in this chapter. In our previous chapter, we established how the theological framework of love and justice provides the impetus for seriously considering injustice, especially racial injustice. In this chapter, we take a deeper dive into understanding one's cultural background, and discuss why this remains a central aspect of working toward love and justice within interdisciplinary work between Christian theology and psychology.

As mentioned in chapter one, culture impacts every person's approach to integration, and this includes authors and scholars. However, when culture is an influence but not explicitly acknowledged, there is a danger that perspectives coming primarily from privileged spaces are considered to be the only normative or right perspectives. In this chapter, we will encourage you to own your

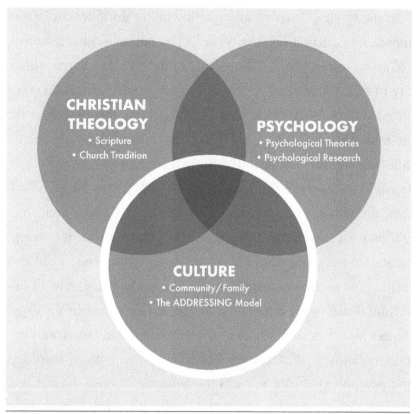

Figure 4.1. Culture in the Integration Triad

cultural story as you practice integration, since your voice and your story matter at the integration table. As mentioned in our first chapter, integration (just like theology) is not just for scholars with PhDs. You already have thoughts about God, self, and others, and your research and study in psychology also brings something important to the conversation. A part of the influence in your perspectives is your cultural and family heritage, which play an important role in how you understand psychology and God. Thus, integration is shaped by the God-given diversity of culture, church traditions, and family traditions.

In the spirit of owning and naming cultural influences in our approach to integration, here we reflect on our own cultural stories. I (Carissa) am a Chinese-Indonesian raised in the metropolitan city of Jakarta, with all nine years of my higher education completed in the United States. Because of this, I find myself navigating the multiplicity of cultures that have influenced and continue to influence my life. Being in the liminal (or in-between) space of multiple cultures is a unique experience that forces me to reflect critically on my cultural influences. Inevitably, I approach integration with these many influences. However, in my own developmental journey, there have been times in my life when I did not realize how certain experiences or cultural identities were an important factor in my integrative formation. For example, my experiences as a cisgender woman, my socioeconomic status, and my able-bodiedness all shape my thinking in integration, theology, and psychology, and it impacts the authors I choose to read and allow to influence my thinking. In growing toward a more mature integrated person, I strive to become increasingly aware of these influences in my writing, teaching, and practice, so as to recognize the limits in my worldviews, and remain cognizant of the multiplicity of experiences that shape our perspectives. These concepts will be fleshed out further in chapters five and six.

For me (William), when I think of identity and cultural background, I think about my upbringing in Texas, which was influenced by a particular type of culture that is unique to Texas. I also think about how I primarily occupied White spaces until I moved to Los Angeles in my twenties. While I went to a large public high school in Texas with a diverse student body, students did not integrate much, and White students largely kept to themselves.

I understand now that this is common. For instance, Graham et al. (2014) demonstrated that adolescent students can benefit from diversity on their school campuses, but this largely depends on students actually taking advantage of opportunities to make friendships outside of their own racial and ethnic groups. Just because students are exposed to diversity doesn't mean that students actually benefit from this diversity within their school settings (Pettigrew, 1998).

As a White, cisgender, heterosexual, and able-bodied male, I've had a lot of privilege in navigating many different spaces throughout my years. However, growing up, I was fairly unaware of elements of my White identity and privilege, and I've had much to learn (and still have much to learn) in regard to White identity and what this has to do with the integration of my Christian faith and psychology. If you identify as White and are reading this book, there might be some aspects of the culture narrative found here that will be new or challenging. That's okay. Just know that some of this work might be hard or feel uncomfortable. However, we want to encourage you that it takes a bit of courage to step into some of these spaces to have a conversation about culture and integration. It's also important to remember that White folks often don't question beliefs regarding our cultural identity until we have a jarring experience that causes us to do so. In fact, in North America, White cultural privilege is so prevalent and comfortable that White people often don't recognize it. White culture can create the illusion that "I don't have a culture." This is why recent research in psychology related to intellectual humility is so important. Intellectual humility is characterized by being grounded in one's beliefs complemented with an openness to critique, as well as understanding differing and even opposing ideas (Deffler et al., 2016; Gregg & Mahadevan, 2014). Addressing culture and recognizing cultural influences with humility and grace is a needed emphasis and focus for shaping our integrative views that we have dedicated further chapters on. White folks cannot ignore the conversation on culture or race, especially within integration circles, because it impacts our theology and psychology, whether we admit this or not. In the past, the integration dialogue within psychology and Christianity has been primarily occupied by voices that are White and male, which simply means that there are a lot of other voices that we must listen to within our dialogue about integration.

Ultimately, we'd like to emphasize that examining cultural elements and our ethnic/racial identity and working to hear and understand the cultural stories of others is really about learning how to love others well. Understanding the cultural element of our integration story is important work for us to do, since it shapes our views and the ways that we relate to God, self, and others. We cannot work toward justice or loving others well, if we haven't been humble enough to slow down and listen to the cultural stories of others and reflect on our own cultural story. We need to move into this cultural work with love, courage, and patience. A more active push toward justice and love within the field of integration involves listening to others who have been negatively affected by systemic racism and creating space to share power and learn from others. When we consider that integration is culturally embedded, our hope is we can help you reflect further on how your own culture has played a part in how you see the world, interpret Scripture, and view God, others, and yourself.

This chapter is focused on the culture component of our Integration Triad; specifically, how culture is embedded in every aspect of our experience of being an embodied human person. In the first section of this chapter, we will address common misconceptions about culture in order to clarify what we mean when we use the word *culture* in this book. We will also give further description as to why it's essential to consider the culture storyline of our Integration Triad. Next, we turn to establishing the theological basis for why being mindful of culture is important to the integration dialogue. Finally, we'll provide some tools to help you deeply reflect on the cultural stories that you already embody.

Myths About Culture

Myth #1: Cultural differences are visible. (Fact: 90% of culture is invisible.) When you think about culture, what comes to mind? For some, images may come to mind that can be considered customs, including what people wear regularly (such as a hanbok, cheongsam, or changshan) or religious attire, such as a hijab. Foods that are stereotypically reflective of localities may also come to mind, as well as language and courtesies (e.g., the way people greet each other, whether it be bowing or kissing both sides of the face). For some people, thinking of cultural differences may initially bring images and thoughts of these visible differences.

Edward T. Hall (1976), an anthropologist and crosscultural researcher, argues that the visible aspects make up just a small part of culture (see figure 4.2). In fact, only 10% of culture is what we call visible culture, while 90% of culture is made of *invisible* factors, including principles, values, priorities, and assumptions

(Comas-Díaz, 2011). When we think of just the visible aspects of culture, it is easy to fall into the trap of believing that we are *acultural*, that we do not have a cultural identity, or that our cultures do not matter. For example, "I do not wear traditional clothing; therefore, I am largely acultural," or "I eat pizza and burgers just like most people I know; therefore, I don't have a culture." For some of you reading this book, you may feel that the topic of culture does not really apply to you, and you may feel that you do not have strong cultural influences. If this is you, consider Edward T. Hall's (1976) statement that our own culture is often *most invisible to ourselves*. So, for those who might not feel like they have a culture, it is important to consider Hall's perspective carefully. That is, sometimes our own culture is most invisible to us, and we often do not realize that we have values and priorities that are particular to our cultural context until we encounter cultural differences.

To describe the invisible nature of our cultural stories, Daniel D. Lee at Fuller Theological Seminary uses an analogy of a fish in water (Lee, 2022). To use Lee's analogy, imagine yourself as a fish living in a pond, and someone asks you to describe the water you're swimming in. If you were a fish, this would certainly be very difficult to do, because the water around you is all you've known. To a fish, the water is invisible since it is simply part of daily experience. It is often the same as a human person who "swims" in a culture. Our culture is like water around us, and it is often invisible to us without further reflection. Yet, the cultural water we swim in consists of values that go back generations. Also, our own particular cultural water consists of stories about our families and our localities (how you are perceived in your current localities, the stereotypes placed on you because of your social identities, etc.). The water you're swimming in has both historical and contextual components. The historical components are the stories that shaped your ancestry and heritage before you were born, and the contextual components are events, both local and global, that impact your life, including socio-political climates (which certainly has a history as well). All of these things, whether we realize it or not, shape who we are as individuals, and the way we see the world, ourselves, and our relationships.

Many of you may remember the first time you had a roommate in college, and suddenly realizing that you have ways of doing things that are very particular to your familial culture, down to very mundane and small things, such as which way you put the water glasses in the cabinet: right side up or upside down. Of course, this is a very small example, simply to highlight that we have ways of doing things that we are often attached to, without realizing that it is particular to our context. However, these assumptions go deeper into much more important things that impact our thinking about integration, such as how we perceive psychological health (Comas-Díaz, 2011). For example, what we consider to be an emotionally healthy person or what we consider psychological well-being is dependent on cultural factors (Comas-Díaz, 2011). The invisible part of our culture is very important to reflect on as a way of honoring values and principles that matter to us (whether we realize it or not), and so we are aware of differences in cultural values. As students who are training to go into psychological fields, it's important to reflect on your cultural values and how they impact what you consider to be psychological health.

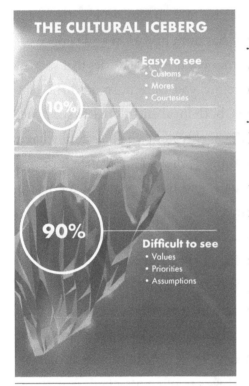

THE CULTURAL ICEBERG

Easy to see
• Customs
• Mores
• Courtesies

10%

90%

Difficult to see
• Values
• Priorities
• Assumptions

Figure 4.2. The cultural iceberg. *Source:* Adapted from Edward T. Hall, *Beyond Culture* (1976)

Myth #2: Culture is defined as a list of behaviors and characteristics. (Fact: Culture is dynamic and fluid.) One of the more harmful ideas, especially in clinical practice, is the idea that cultural competence means mastering knowledge of discrete traits and characteristics of ethnic minority groups (Tervalon & Murray-Garcia, 1998). Early trainings on multicultural competence (mostly from the early 2000s and before) have modules or chapters that describe characteristics of certain ethnic minority groups and how to work with them in clinical settings. This approach is simplistic and perpetuates stereotyping, partially because it assumes that culture is static, that it does not change (Hunt, 2001). It also assumes homogeneity among its members (also called *ethnic gloss,* Trimble & Dickson, 2005, as cited in APA, 2017), implying that all members of a similar ethnic group possess these same characteristics. As Hunt (2001) suggests, it is more helpful to think about culture as both a collection of ideas that individuals access in making sense of their experiences, and a collection of possible actions that determines behavior. With this definition of culture, we are reminded that culture is dynamic, versatile, and expresses itself in a variety of ways among its members (Hunt, 2001).

Take a moment to reflect on how you may interact or communicate when you are with close friends you have known since childhood, compared to when you are in a new workplace or meeting coworkers for the first time. How you are described in these two contexts may reflect very distinct characteristics even though you are the same person with the same set of values and priorities. Another example is language. A person who speaks multiple languages (both fluently) may act somewhat differently (more extroverted, more emotive) when speaking one language over another. (Some of you who speak multiple languages may identify with this!) The APA Multicultural Guidelines (2017) acknowledge this by stating that psychologists who are multilingual should consider following the client's lead on what language they would like to use in the therapeutic encounter. Citing evidence presented in Javier (2007), the guidelines (2017) state that clients recounting an experience may find that their emotions are more accessible when speaking of an experience in one language over another. For the therapist to insist on only using one language in therapy would run the risk of missing very important nonverbal, affective meanings in the experience. Another important aspect of the fluidity of culture is how cultural identity develops across the life stages (APA, 2017). The cultural identity that might feel most salient to you when you were a child may be different from the cultural identity that feels salient now. Or perhaps, when you were a child, the term *culture* did not carry much meaning for you, but as you move to a different neighborhood or start in a new school or college, you may encounter cultural differences that cause you to reflect more on your cultural identity.

Myth #3: Culture is defined by a person's race or ethnicity. (Fact: Culture is an intersection of multiple aspects of identity.) *How does psychology define culture?* In 2017, APA updated its Multicultural Guidelines from its earlier 2002 version (APA, 2002). One of the most significant changes was the lens by which culture was viewed. The original guideline emphasized race and ethnicity as a focus of the guidelines (APA, 2002). The updated 2017 version shifted to a definition which is broader and more fully takes into account the complexity of culture, to include: "language, gender, race, ethnicity, ability status, sexual orientation, age, gender identity, socioeconomic status, religion, spirituality, immigration status, education, and employment, among other variables" (APA, 2017). In this book, when we use the term *culture*, we are referring to the intersection of multiple facets of a person's identity including the above factors.

One of the widely referenced models in conceptualizing cultural complexity is Pamela Hays's (2008) ADDRESSING framework. ADDRESSING stands for Age, Developmental and acquired Disabilities, Religion, Ethnicity, Socioeconomic status, Sexual orientation, Indigenous heritage, National origin, and Gender (2008). When we only conceptualize culture from the lens of ethnicity and race, we miss out on very important experiences and meaning-making repertoire that often relate to how we think about psychology and our faith. This concept was first introduced in the field of law by Kimberlé Crenshaw (1989) using the term *intersectionality*. In her paper (1989), she argues that when we only look at experiences of Black individuals in the workplace, for example, we miss important nuances (which include multiple oppressive and discriminatory experiences) that Black *women* experience. Intersectionality is an important concept we discuss toward the end of this chapter, especially as you apply the concept to your own stories. Here, we simply wish to introduce it to clarify that when we refer to culture, we do not mean a single dimension of cultural identity, but to acknowledge at minimum the intersection of factors in the ADDRESSING framework mentioned above (2008).

How does the Bible define culture? Having established this definition of culture from APA, here, we would also like to note some other contributions to the topic by theologians and biblical scholars.

Ethnicity is a term that is found in Scripture (Hebrew: *goy* or *am*; Greek: *ethnos*). Ethnicity refers to one's identification of group identity, heritage, language, common ancestry, and common group experience over time (Harper, 2016; Manickam, 2008). Ethnicity, as Lisa Sharon Harper rightly points out, is good and is created by God (Harper, 2016, p. 140).

Culture is implicit in Scripture, but the word itself is never used. Culture is a sociological and anthropological term that refers to the beliefs, norms, rituals, arts, and worldviews of particular people groups in a particular place at a particular time. Culture is fluid (Harper, 2016, p. 140).

Nationality indicates the sovereign nation-state where an individual is a legal citizen. Many English translations of the Bible translate the Hebrew and Greek words for ethnicity as "nation." However, nation-states did not exist prior to the late eighteenth century and are modern constructs (Harper, 2016). Before the modern era, people organized themselves around ethnic tribes, clans, and ethnically based empires (Harper, 2016, pp. 140-41).

Race is a form of classification and labeling of human beings that is imposed by a society or a people group based on appearance, like skin color, facial features, and hair type (Manickam, 2008). Racial categories are imposed by others, and we have little control on how others see us or classify us. Racism exists when racial categories become the way that humans are assigned worth and value (Manickam, 2008). And some, like pastor and theologian Joseph Barndt, have argued that it is both prejudice combined with power that creates racism (Barndt, 2011). Racial categories continue to hold power since they have been used to guide decisions regarding how to allocate resources. Racial categories do change over time, but only as governments refine language (Harper, 2016, p. 146).[1]

In this book, we draw from the above psychological and biblical definitions of culture as follows: culture is defined as "beliefs, norms, rituals, arts, and worldviews of particular people groups" (Harper, 2016, p. 140), influenced by the intersection of our multiple facets of identity (APA, 2017). One aspect that is not explicitly addressed in both of these definitions is locality. We will describe locality in more detail in this chapter, but for now, it is sufficient to note that in contrast to biblical times when people groups moved through time and space relatively together, we live in a time of great mobility and globalization. Many individuals or nuclear families leave their ethnic groups to go to a locality in which many in their surroundings do not share their ethnicity, language, or nationality. Locality, we would argue, has a strong influence on what we define as our *culture*, and it evolves over time. Within locality is the construct of race. Race itself is not an inherent construct but

---

[1]For more on how racial definitions have changed in US history see Harper, L. S. (2016). *The very good gospel: How everything wrong can be made right*. WaterBrook Press, pp. 140-66.

rather, is imposed on us by our society (Harper, 2016). These imposed perceptions impact the way others see us and how we feel about ourselves, group identity, and well-being. We will discuss this further and in broader terms in the section titled "Intersectionality and Locality."

Key Concept 4.1

Culture really does matter for Christian theology.

At this point, some of you may be wondering, but what does all this have to do with our spiritual life or faith experiences? Does culture really matter in our spiritual lives or engagement with God? Does God relate to us as cultural beings? Many authors (Warren Brown and Brad Strawn, Daniel D. Lee, J. Kameron Carter, Al Dueck, Steven Sandage and Jeanine Brown, and Alexander Jun and colleagues, among others) have addressed this question, and below we draw on their work. Ultimately, these authors argue that to ignore cultural embeddedness is in fact an infraction to the design God has intended for us.

Cultural Embeddedness from Theological Viewpoints

Jesus' Jewish identity. Let's begin by considering Jesus and his cultural identity. Jesus was a Jew. He was born to Jewish parents, and his Jewish lineage was meticulously detailed in the Gospel of Matthew (1:1-17). Jesus was raised within Jewish customs and was thoroughly embedded in Jewish culture.

Jesus was raised a Jew and lived his life as such. He is called Yeshua, a common Jewish name. Consistent with Jewish culture, he was circumcised on the eighth day, presented to God in the temple (Luke 2:22), and a simple sacrifice of two turtledoves was offered (Luke 2:24). Jesus was raised according to the Law (Luke 2:39), celebrated Passover (Luke 2:41), kept the Sabbath (Luke 4:16), approved tithing (Matthew 23:23) and sacrifice and voluntary gifts at the temple (Mark 12:41-44), gave thanks before meals (Deuteronomy 8:10; John 6:11), wore tassels on his garments (Matthew 9:20), and tended to avoid contact with the Gentiles (Matthew 10:6). In following the Mosaic tradition (Exodus 20:17; Deuteronomy 5:21) and the Prophets (Isaiah 29:13), Jesus places importance on motive and intention (Mark 7:8).

The Gospels make painstaking effort in describing his cultural embeddedness in his Jewish identity and participation in Jewish customs and community. While the Gospels contextualize Jesus and his Jewish identity, Western Christianity over the years has emphasized an amorphous spiritual being who is stripped of his culture, context, lineage, and history. In fact, many iconic images of Jesus portray him as White, with blond hair and blue eyes (Merritt, 2013; see figure 4.3). This goes back in history to the Middle Ages and Renaissance eras, and potentially even earlier (Jun et al., 2018). Some of these artistic expressions were driven by an emphasis on Christ's purity, which in the West has historically been depicted with light colors (Merritt, 2013). In attempts to spiritualize Jesus, icons and images that dominate Western Christianity portray him as a man disembodied from his Jewishness, detached from his actual historical context and ethnic identity. It is important to note that in contrast to the Western representation of Jesus, many historical accounts describe Jesus as an average Jewish man (Merritt, 2013; see figure 4.4).

When Jesus Christ is abstracted from his cultural heritage and detached from his incarnated cultural embodiment, as J. Kameron Carter (2008) aptly notes, we end up projecting our own cultural values onto Jesus. In North America and many other parts of the world, these projected cultural values consist of Western Eurocentric sentiments, dispositions, and values.

Figure 4.3. *Figure of Christ* by German painter Heinrich Hofmann, 1884

Western dualistic thinking and its impact on Christian theology. Western dualism is one of the results of the Enlightenment and modernity. When we refer to Western dualism here, we are referring to the tendency in both Christian thought and contemporary society to separate the mind or soul from the body. The outcome of Western dualism is an "essentially rationalist conception of human being" where humans are related to each other by their minds more than any other aspect of one's personal being (Gunton, 2005, p. 49). If reason is the focus of what makes a human, then *relations*

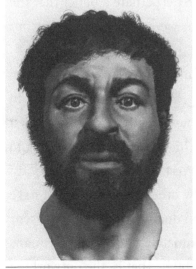

Figure 4.4. Computer-generated image based on the skull of a Jewish man of the first century

between humans is not constitutive of true personhood (Gunton, 2005). Dualistic thinking has also been present within some Christian thinking, and while there is a long history here that we don't have space to cover, the tendency is still present in some Christian churches to emphasize the spiritual aspects of human life and downplay or disregard the bodily aspects of our human experience.[2] As a result, some Western Christian theological reflection has had the tendency to describe persons as having a separate spiritual soul that is distinct from the body, and to describe humans apart from their cultural context. However, Western dualism neglects the fact that our bodies, hearts, and minds are intricately connected. Brown and Strawn (2012) similarly note that many Christians have come to believe that we simply have a body, whereas in reality we are embodied creatures and we "*are* bodies" (p. 4). In Christian churches and Bible studies, it is very common to ask each other, "What is going on with your heart?" and implicitly we perpetuate a belief that the heart is a "spiritual" aspect of who we are, separate from our lived, embodied experience.

One of the major proponents of modernity's Western dualism is René Descartes, famous for saying, "I think, therefore, I am." In this statement, it is clear that the primary faculty of a person is their reasoning capacity that is held in a hierarchy over the body and emotions. The first problem with Western dualism is the body-mind (soul) split, but there are a few other byproducts that have come from it. Not only does Western dualism emphasize a disembodied spiritual state, but it also ultimately understands humans in an individualistic way (Gunton, 2005). That is, the outworking

---

[2] For a review of this history, see further C. E. Gunton (2005) and C. Taylor (1989).

of Western dualism is the understanding that humans are assumed primarily autonomous (vs. relational), and mostly rational/
cognitive (vs. emotional).[3]

This problem is related to how Jesus' Jewish identity has been
de-emphasized in Western Christianity, the point we have outlined above. As we look back in church history, we are reminded
that conceptualizing Jesus and ourselves primarily as amorphous
and disembodied spiritual beings is actually a heresy, under the
loose label of what we might understand as Gnosticism (Carter,
2008). This second-century heresy, Gnosticism, held that there
were spiritual and material realms to the universe, with the spiritual realm being good, while the material and bodily realm was
evil (Mirecki, 2000). The early church father Irenaeus was very
vocal in fighting against this heresy in the second century, and
his primary argument is that if Jesus became incarnate and appeared to us in the flesh, then nothing that is bodily or material
can be disregarded as unimportant or evil (Farrow, 1995). As
such, to elevate the spiritual over the material, or worse, to ignore
Christ's embodiment in his flesh, is to dismiss God's loving af-
firmation of his material creation (Carter, 2008). When Christian
writings (especially in Western Christianity) privilege the spiritual inner life and rarely unpack how our spirituality plays out
in our God-given embodiedness (gender, race, ability, age), we
are repeating what Irenaeus fought hard to correct in early
church history.

---

[3]Our emotional life is very important, and we would benefit from paying attention to our body
and our physiological reactions in giving us important information about ourselves. Some of you
may have seen Amy Cuddy's TED talk (2012), where she described the experiment that people
who were asked to bite a pencil (and therefore, forced to smile) reported feeling happy. The
James-Lange Theory even states that our emotions are just an interpretation of our bodily
reactions.

So, How Does Culture Relate to Integration?

The way we relate to God is highly influenced by our cultures. As we have seen, Jesus was deeply embedded in his own Jewish cultural context with traditions, rituals, and values. Over the history of the church, we have sometimes forgotten about these culturally Jewish components that make up the very life of Christ. As mentioned in our first chapters, one's own religious and theological tradition is shaped and expressed within our familial and communal cultural context. In reflecting on this, we are reminded that culture and Christian theology cannot be completely separated, and that is why both are emphasized as important elements of the Integration Triad. We have also seen that in the history of the Western church, we have favored certain assumptions about Jesus (e.g., light-skinned, light-eyed depictions), in addition to favoring certain assumptions of human nature that divorce the spiritual from the embodied elements of human personhood.

A worship service from a particular church denomination in Los Angeles can be very different from the way that same church denomination worships in Buenos Aires, for example. Traditions have rituals, rites, and values that make up a culture, and cultures are often influenced by the community's conceptualization of the divine and how the divine relates to humanity. In actively conceptualizing integration as culturally embedded, the integration literature would become more reflective of the body of Christ in its cultural and denominational diversity.

One of the most influential writings in psychology of religion is Gordon Allport's intrinsic and extrinsic religiosity. Intrinsic religiosity is defined as a motivation toward one's identified religion due to having a strong faith in its beliefs (Allport & Ross, 1967).

Extrinsic religiosity, on the other hand, is defined as a motivation toward a religion for its social benefits and because it provides comfort, among other reasons (Allport & Ross, 1967). Psychological literature highlights intrinsic religiosity as the better version of the two; however, it has now become clear that the valuing of beliefs is more reflective of a Protestant religious value. Cohen and Hill (2007) have since found that Jews, Catholics, and Protestants express their religiosity differently on the intrinsic-extrinsic continuum. While Protestants largely endorse intrinsic religiosity, Jews and Catholics tended to be more "collectivistically grounded" and emphasized communal aspects and rituals in their religious practices (Cohen & Hill, 2007). Literature that is predominated by Protestant writings only represents a narrow slice of Christianity and an even narrower slice of religiosity, with the importance of communal practices and rituals often left out of the conversation (Cohen & Hill, 2007). Thus, when we consider our particular Christian tradition, and our theological beliefs and practices, it is important to keep in mind how different traditions have varying degrees of emphasis on individual beliefs and communal practices.

Key Concept 4.2

Developing our own integrative identity includes reflecting on our cultural stories and naming our cultural influences.

As mentioned above, culture, as the water we swim in, is often invisible to us. And yet, the process of naming our influences is so important, both in honoring the stories that God has weaved into our lives, and in moving toward maturity as adults and professionals. On the latter point, as we interact with people who come from and swim in different waters, having an awareness of our own cultural water is key to understanding differences.

For me (William), more intentional reflection about my own culture and cultural differences did not occur until I was a young adult. In fact, for many folks who identify as White in the United States, there is often a denial that being White carries with it any cultural implications at all. For me, it wasn't really until I moved to Los Angeles in my midtwenties that I was forced to give a more careful examination of my own cultural identity. One very helpful piece that I read early on was Peggy McIntosh's (2003) article "White Privilege: Unpacking the Invisible Knapsack," where McIntosh identifies twenty-six elements of White privilege that she noticed frequently in her life over the course of time. These include items like, "If a traffic cop pulls me over or if the IRS audits my tax return, I can be sure I haven't been singled out because of my race" (McIntosh, 2003, p. 193). Another one she notes is, "Whether I use checks, credit cards, or cash, I can count on my skin color not to work against the appearance of financial reliability" (McIntosh, 2003, p. 192). Reading through all twenty-six of these items helped me realize that I had enjoyed certain privileges that were not the experience of BIPOC (Black, Indigenous, and Persons of Color).

Not very long after I had read this article, I was driving in my car and was late for a meeting. While stuck in traffic, I decided to cross over to the carpool lane at a point where it was illegal to enter. By doing this, I broke two laws—I entered the lane illegally, and was driving by myself in a lane that was reserved for two people. I had only been driving in the carpool lane a few seconds when I saw flashing lights behind me and a police officer on a motorcycle instructed me to pull over. Once I had pulled off on the shoulder of the freeway, a White male police officer came up to the window. "Do you know why I pulled you over?" he asked. "Yes," I answered sheepishly. I also knew the ticket for this was going to be steep.

"Look, carpool lanes are for two people or more. You know, I've seen lots of accidents doing exactly what you did. But today I'm gonna let you off with a warning. Be more careful in the future."

My initial reaction was one of shock. He didn't ask for my license. No registration check. I was expecting a large ticket (which I deserved) but was let off with a warning. I drove carefully to my destination feeling pretty thankful that I had gotten off so easy.

The next day I was talking with one of my friends who was African American and told him the story about being pulled over and let off with a warning. To be honest, I hadn't thought much more about it. I casually shared the experience and chalked it up to being lucky. I was caught off guard as he became frustrated. "No, William. It's not that you're lucky; it's because you're White. When Black men get pulled over, they might not just get a warning—they're often afraid for their life." My friend proceeded to tell me how his mom first gave him "the talk" when he was little about what it means to be a Black male in America. One of those things included in that talk as he got older was that you should always follow all traffic laws very carefully to avoid getting pulled over by the police—but sometimes you might even get pulled by the police for doing nothing wrong.

I realized that I had lived with the privilege of not being afraid of the police if I got pulled over. If I did get pulled over, I didn't think much about whether or not it was because of my race.

There was never a talk that my parents gave me because they were afraid that if I was pulled over by the police, it could lead to my death. I never had feared that reaching for my wallet or cell phone would bring aggressive action from a police officer. This stands in stark contrast to the deadly force that the police often use during traffic stops against unarmed Black men. The senseless and tragic deaths like those of Philando Castile, Duante Wright, and Walter Scott are painful reminders of how quickly police traffic stops can turn violent.

Remember how the water of our culture that we swim in is often invisible to us? This aspect of my culture was invisible to me until I encountered a friend who was honest enough to help me see that my experience was not the experience of everyone. It's also worth noting that my friend was most likely doing something that was emotionally exhausting for him (i.e., having to educate a White male on aspects of privilege). Now I can see that he was doing it to help me become more aware of my own lived reality and White privilege. I grew from this experience, and God used it to help me recognize how much privilege often goes unnoticed until we are confronted with a situation that makes us see it. I began to see White privilege in other places in my life too as I began to reflect more deeply on it.

Especially if you identify as White, there might also be moments that feel uncomfortable as you begin to recognize aspects of your own culture and see disparities in how others have been treated. At this point we encourage you to be open to this exploration of culture as an opportunity—an opportunity to learn from others, to learn how to love others well, and an opportunity to learn from God. In essence, becoming good integrators in regards to culture means that we move toward effective collaborations and ensure that we do not impose the assumptions of our cultural water on those who live in different cultural realities. This is especially true when we are in positions of power (e.g., as therapists, medical doctors, teachers, professors). Being careful not to impose our own cultural assumptions on others is part of what Sandage and colleagues call *mature alterity*, defined as "healthy and virtuous capacities to relate effectively across sociocultural and other differences combined with an authentic commitment to social justice" (An et al., 2019, p. 128; Sandage & Brown, 2018; Sandage & Harden, 2011). Sandage and Brown also note (2018) that mature alterity naturally involves "high levels of intercultural competence and a commitment to social justice" (p. 180).

Mature alterity, in our view (and we believe Sandage and colleagues would agree), is an ongoing developmental process—just like our views of integration are an ongoing developmental process. We do not *arrive* at mature alterity—the engagement in the ongoing growth process is a part of what requires maturity. In moving toward an ongoing growth in mature alterity, we go through a process of examining our assumptions as they have been shaped by our cultures. For instance, in my (William's) story above about the traffic stop, some reflection happened in the moment with my friend, but more reflection and insight was gained after the conversation was over as I continued to ask questions about my own cultural experiences and elements of White privilege. Also, for those that identify as White and might have a hard time thinking of what White culture consists of for you, noting some of the privileges that have come with being White can be a good place to start. For this, we would encourage you to read McIntosh's article "White Privilege" in order to aid in some of your reflection.

The Stories of Our Community

Our family stories. With the above process in mind, let's dive into the core of our cultural stories: *the stories of our community*. In its most narrow sense, our community consists of our family. These are the stories that were told to you when you were young, perhaps over and over again. In my (Carissa's) family, these include stories about overcoming difficulties during war time; stories of how my maternal grandmother, who only had a second-grade formal education, overcame odds and became an entrepreneur who ensured that all of her grandchildren had a college education. Each of these stories carries familial values and messages of who I am; the cloth I am made from, so to speak. These are stories of resilience that keep me going in moments of challenges, remind me of my values, and the stories that I plan on passing on to my children. Many of you likely also have stories about your family that have been shared across the generations that remind you of your family's values and traits. Values and stories often go hand in hand, as was the case in Jesus' use of stories and parables in his teachings.

ADDRESSING as culture. Outside of our family, each of us belongs to other communities, which include friends, churches, college campuses, workplaces. Each of these communities has their own subcultures. While these subcultures certainly influence who we are, here we wish to address even larger communities that influence us, that we may not even realize we are a part of. These are communities with whom we share our ADDRESSING factors. We will illustrate how these ADDRESSING factors can constitute a culture, focusing on the first factor, age. Age is conceptualized in the ADDRESSING model as having two different components: the first is age range and stages of life, and the second, generational influence. In making references to groups of people with shared generational influences, we use terms such as baby boomers, generation X, millennials, generation Z, and generation Alpha. While these terms have been used with overgeneralization and stereotyping, each generation shares national and global events at similar life stages, which impact their values and thinking. The APA Multicultural Guidelines states: "The historical period one lives through may also affect how individuals perceive themselves. Growing up during the Great Depression had a lifelong effect on the lives of those in later adolescence at the time, but only a minimal effect on those who were younger" (Elder, 1974, 1998, as cited in APA, 2017, p. 77). While you certainly may not feel that you are a part of a community with everyone in your age range, there are shared communal experiences that you have in your particular generation.

In addition to generational influences, our age range and stages of life involve a certain set of beliefs, values, assumptions, and priorities. One way to think about this is from Erik Erikson's stages—adults between the ages of eighteen and forty, for example, have a developmental priority of establishing a sense of connection and intimacy with not just romantic partners, but also in friendships and among family members. In the next stage of ages forty to sixty-five, the developmental priority changes to establishing generativity, investing in future generations and establishing legacy in the world. In each of these stages, how we choose to invest our time and resources, may change along with our age range and developmental stage, highlighting further the concept that our cultural identity is dynamic. With these changes, the way we understand psychology and experience our spirituality may shift as well. Our experiences often inform how we understand God, psychological variables, and who we are as cultural beings. So this is what we mean when we speak of those who share your intersectional identity as a community of sorts: those with whom you have some shared experiences due to a shared identity. Each generation and each life stage has a culture of its own, and again (as addressed in Myth #2), when we say the group has a culture, we do not mean they all behave the same way. However, they have similar experiences and priorities that inform the reservoir from which each individual makes meaning and determines actions (Hunt, 2001). In other words, each dimension of the ADDRESSING factors carries a tide of cultural influences on its members through shared collective experiences.

Intersectionality. In the above section, we discussed the ADDRESSING factor as individual factors with its unique potential shared experiences. We dissected an individual aspect (age) of the ADDRESSING framework to illustrate how each of these aspects can constitute a shared experience among its members, and create a culture among them. In our journey to becoming more aware of our own culture and that of others, however, we do not only focus on one cultural factor of the ADDRESSING model. Earlier in the chapter, we referenced Crenshaw's (1989) initial paper on intersectionality, which highlights discriminatory experiences uniquely experienced by Black women, as contrasted with White women (if we are only looking at race) and as compared to Black men (if we are only looking at the dimension of gender). Intersectionality, "by its broadest definition, incorporates the vast array of cultural, structural, sociobiological, economic, and social contexts by which individuals are shaped and with which they identify" (Howard & Renfrow, 2014, as cited in APA, 2017, p. 19), and highlights group differences that exist within each social category. APA states that "individuals' perspectives are shaped by the multiplicity of identities and contexts to which they belong" (APA, 2017, p. 20). Each of these intersecting experiences has an impact on what we notice in our environment, how we feel and think about ourselves, others, psychology, and our experiences with God.

Intersectionality and locality. As we consider the ADDRESSING factors, it is important to note that our intersectional identity is not just individual experiences; in fact, our identity and how we experience ourselves and our social milieu is largely shaped by systemic oppression and experiences of discrimination (Adames et al., 2018). This relates to what we refer to above as the interactions between our ADDRESSING factors and our localities. For example, Adames et al. (2018) shares the story of an Afro-Latinx who immigrated from Colombia, stating that in the United States, people often mistake him as Indian or African American. This creates feelings of loneliness for him as he is not seen in his cultural identity (Adames et al., 2018). In Harper's (2016) definition above, this client was often perceived within the *race* construct (externally imposed), not his true *ethnic* identity (inherently defined).

When we zoom out and consider the larger picture, we see that our ADDRESSING factors also interact with various systemic oppressions in localities, typically labeled as *-isms*. For example, a person's experience of their age and generational identity is likely to be influenced by ageism. If an elderly person is often treated as if they are forgetful or frail, this shapes their experiences of themselves and how they relate to others in their world. So is the case with ableism. With ableism, we can see even more clearly how our physical environment can exclude or add distress for people with disabilities. With each added difficulty, distress, and feeling of exclusion (i.e., this environment was not created for people like me), one's relationship with one's identity is impacted.

There are other -isms, including racism (discrimination based on skin color or phenotype), ethnocentrism (discrimination based on ethnicities), nativism (discrimination based on immigration status; Adames et al., 2018). Consistent with the concept of intersectionality, it is best if we think of the various -isms that influence our lives in our identities, as opposed to only focusing on one aspect. For example, an immigrant with disability might consider how nativism and ableism intersect to influence their well-being and experiences of their identity (Adames et al., 2018). As you think about these, you may be feeling emotions coming up for you; whether it be sadness or lament for the various discriminations that exist in our global and local societies, or perhaps you are feeling anger or numbness. At this point, we encourage you to pause and take note of your feelings. Write them down so you can come back to it later.

Wrapping Things Up

By stating that integration is culturally embedded we mean that our integration story is shaped by our faith traditions, our cultural backgrounds, our understanding of key aspects of Scripture, and our own interests and knowledge of psychology. Since integration is culturally embedded—this means that it is always personal, local, as well as being a communal exercise. As mentioned earlier, each of us brings all the summative experiences of our lives, church background, understanding of God, and knowledge of psychology to the table when we practice integration. This is what makes the task of integration a rich and diverse experience. Your own family norms and systems, your cultural and denominational traditions, and your own interpretations of key aspects of Scripture will all inform your study of the discipline.

Understanding that integration is culturally embedded acknowledges that our interpretation of Scripture and our interests in psychology are influenced by our culture, gender, family norms, and life experiences. Jenny Pak (Yangarber-Hicks et al., 2006) argues that to exclude culture from the integration of psychology and theology is a failure of examining the whole person. Moreover, an awareness of our own cultural expressions and how these aspects of culture shape our experiences in the world is a vital aspect of spiritual development and formation. Multicultural awareness is part of spiritual formation since it involves not simply tolerating the differences of others but actually recognizing that it will require attentiveness and empathy for both oneself and others.

Reflection Questions

1. What are daily/weekly rituals that are important to you? Why are they important? List values and priorities that may be the driving factor behind these routines.

2. What annual routines are important to you? Think of holiday traditions and what factors have influenced what you do on these holidays. List values and priorities that may be the driving factor behind these routines.

3. Have you encountered a person or a group of people that seems to have very different priorities and values from you? How do you make sense of this experience?

4. What are some signs of a psychologically healthy person? What might influence your thinking about this? To what extent are there overlaps with the way your family, context, and community might think about this topic?

5. Write some of the stories of the people in your family. This may include stories of war time, stories of migration, stories of successes and failures, etc.

6. What are some of the values inherent in these stories? What messages do they convey about what's important to you and your family?

7. How was religion and spirituality treated in the broader culture you grew up in?

8. What are some views you have of psychology that may have been influenced by the culture and context that you grew up in?

9. How have some of these stories or experiences that you have reflected on above shaped the way you think about God, psychology, and the integration of the two?

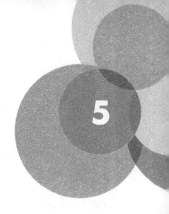

The Cycle of Transformation

Developing Our Integrative Identity

It is extraordinary the way people, music and cultures develop. The paths and experiences that guide them are unpredictable. Shaped by our families, neighborhoods, cultures and countries, each of us ultimately goes through this process of incorporating what we learn with who we are and who we seek to become. As we struggle to find our individual voices, I believe we must look beyond the voice we've been assigned, and find our place among the tones and timbre of human expression.

Yo-Yo Ma (2008)

After I (William) graduated from college, I got a summer job working as an outdoor wilderness instructor at a young adult camp in the Ouachita National Forest in Arkansas.[1] The Ouachita National Forest is about a 1.8 million acre sprawl of rolling hills and

---

[1]Portions of this chapter have also appeared in Dwiwardani & Whitney (2022) and Whitney et al. (2023).

mountains in Arkansas and Oklahoma. As instructors, we would take teenagers on a variety of outdoor trips and teach them basic skills needed for each trip. For instance, on the backpacking trips, we would teach them how to plan out their overnight trip, pack their backpack, set up a tent, and build a fire. On the overnight backpacking trip, we would pack ropes and harnesses, along with the rest of the hardware, and teach some basic rock climbing and rappelling skills.

All of the instructors had to be trained on how to set up and break down the ropes, how to secure everyone into their harnesses, and how to belay a climber. (The term *belay* just means that every rock climber has someone holding the other end of the rope in tension to catch the climber if they fall.) As you might imagine, instructors had to go through training on how to get ropes set up safely and how to go through standard safety checks (always a good idea) before sending someone else's child over the side of a mountain dangling from a rope.

I had already had some experience with tying the various knots that were needed, but this was the first summer that I was on a weekly rotation to be in charge of setting up the rappelling and rock climbing areas. Over the weeks of training, the reality began to set in that I was going to be responsible if the rope knots were not done correctly. The cliffs we rappelled off were around fifty feet high (about a five-story building). We're not talking about Mount Kilimanjaro here, but if a rope knot slipped because I tied it incorrectly and someone fell from that height, it would always mean a very serious injury or possible death. As this new reality of my responsibility set in, my love of rappelling shifted from being fun to being anxiety-inducing and stressful.

Partly because of my anxiety, and partly because I like to do things well, I practiced a lot of knot tying with short pieces of rope in my time off. One of the first things to note about getting trained for rappelling or rock climbing is that book knowledge only takes you so far. For training on how to tie knots (as with so many other hands-on skills), a book description with pictures introduces the idea, but reading about it alone cannot guarantee that you will be able to tie that knot in real life. None of us would feel much comfort from a rock climbing instructor or an airline pilot who announced: "Don't worry, everyone! This is my first time to do this in real life, but I've read a *ton* of books on this, and have memorized everything I need to know." You wouldn't go on that rock-climbing adventure or get in an airplane if someone audaciously announced that level of knowledge of a subject. Thus, there is a huge difference between reading about something in a book, and experiencing something and practicing it in real life. This is the difference between head knowledge and experiential or applied knowledge. Moreover, experiential knowledge of a subject is usually transferred relationally or mediated to us through relationships with other persons. Head knowledge is reading about knot tying in a book; experiential knowledge is the skill of being able to do it in real life when there is a human dangling from the other end of that rope. And, like with a lot of other things in life, you realize the limits of head knowledge when you have to do it in real time.

Experiential knowledge is gained through other people guiding us in a hands-on way through the process. If you understand this difference, you'll understand why we stress in this chapter that reading or theoretical knowledge is part of integration, but not the entire thing. There's also integration that is lived and experienced in our person (i.e., embodied integration) as we actively are changed by God and work toward love and justice. The point of this chapter is that God can use our integration journey to develop our own integrative identity—to help us change, grow, and mature in our spiritual life and become a more integrated person.

Practicing the knots is one thing, but going out into the field and doing it for myself synthesized my knowledge in a new and important way. Reading this book on integration will only get you so far, since integration is not just something we think about, but also impacts how we believe and behave as we gain greater understanding of our faith, cultural identity, and psychology, and work toward loving God and others well.

I practiced those knots using small pieces of rope time and time and time again. I went over it in my mind when I didn't have the ropes in front of me, and when the time came to take my test, I passed it with no problem. However, this first test was just done with small pieces of rope, with no one clipped into the other end. The second level of tests was going out and doing it with the instructors many times.

My first day for the rope setup as the lead instructor occurred on a particularly gray morning. I was unprepared for how anxious I would feel, and was thinking about the twenty excited teenagers that would be lined up in about an hour trusting in my setup and knowledge of the knots and equipment. My palms were sweaty, and I was breathing heavier than normal. I did everything as I had learned and already practiced. Tying the webbing around the tree using the correct knots, I secured the safety line and ropes. After I had done my checks, my climbing partner double-checked everything. "You're good to go," he announced, and gave me a thumbs-up.

The general rule was that whoever did the rope set up was the first one to rappel down. So, I clipped myself in and placed my feet on the edge for the first rappel of the day. If any of you have been rappelling, you know that there's a moment where you stand on the edge and you have to trust your rope and lean waaaay back into the harness so that your center of gravity becomes your seat in the harness. If you don't do this and try to stand up too much, you slam into the side of the cliff. That moment of leaning back and trusting in the rope, equipment, and harness is a snapshot of what faith or trust is, and it's also the real moment where you know that everything about your setup holds. As I leaned back everything felt good, I looked over the side, said a quick prayer, and made my first small jump down the side releasing the rope with my right hand so that I could slide down the rope as I held gently onto it with my left. I descended the side without a problem, and to my great relief everything went fine. Whew! I was relieved. My heart was still beating fast, and I was out of breath, but a sense of accomplishment came as I was at the bottom and I looked up to the top to see my partner give me another thumbs-up. I went back up to the top and went down again, this time feeling like I could enjoy it much more.

Before everyone joined us, we each had time to descend the cliff four or five times, and with each time I grew more confident and had more fun on the way down. While my previous experiences of rappelling had been fun when someone else set things up, there was a whole new skill set of knowledge that was integrated within me that day as the lead instructor. And, more importantly, it was only in doing it myself that I began to learn the particular ways that I needed to improve. I also didn't learn alone. I was taught by others (not just books) and learned through experience and practice. It was the actual practice of it that helped me grow in my knowledge of the subject. Moreover, every time I did rope setup or rope checks, this knowledge became more synthesized and integrated into me as a person. After a while you don't need the book anymore, it becomes part of who you are, and your knowledge of the subject from doing it in real life actually moves beyond what the book could tell you because of all of these tiny bits of practical knowledge that you acquire from actually performing the rope set up in real life.

Just like with my experience of setting up the ropes, there is a transformation that occurs when we try or learn something new. My experience as the lead instructor that day was an experience that challenged and jarred me, but staying present and continuing to learn and practice through the fear and anxiety was what helped me change and grow. It is often these life experiences that press our current level of knowledge of integration and force us to rethink, broaden, or deepen what we have known before.

Key Concept 5.1

Working toward greater love and justice doesn't just happen. It's part of the transformation that occurs as we really sit with our experiences of faith, culture, and psychology and let God's Spirit change us.

This lesson about rope setup isn't unique to this one thing; it is transferable to many other areas where there is information that has to be applied to a real-life situation. In fact, we understand integration to happen as we have these transformative experiences that cause us to think deeply about our faith, psychology, and cultural background. As we move to new ways of understanding our faith, cultural stories, or psychology, we also develop greater capacities to work toward love and justice—which is the subject of this chapter.

For instance, we may learn in class the five bullet points of practicing empathy and see a Venn Diagram that describes good listening skills with a client in psychotherapy, but it's another thing when we see our first client and feel that anxiety and tension in our stomach. We may watch our instructor in psychology class demonstrate how to do data analysis and completely understand it while we are in class, but when we try it on our own it's a different story, and we get confused, or miss a smaller step along the way. Interdisciplinary work between psychology and Christianity works in the same way. The integration of psychology and Christian theology can be presented as a topic to be thought about in a class, where we can learn its contours and different methods and models, but it's a whole different thing as we let ourselves be changed by our integrative reflection and we eventually develop new ways of thinking and behaving through reflection on our faith, psychology, and cultural identity. As we have argued, we believe integration is best practiced when we bring all of who we are to the table and begin to reflect with others on our faith, culture, and studies in psychology. As we are changed, we also develop new capacities to love and work toward justice in our church, communities, and society. Integration isn't just head knowledge that we acquire through a book or an assignment in class. It is something that we embody in new ways through life experiences as God's Spirit upholds and empowers us.

Developing Our Integrative Identity:
Starting Where We Are

Whenever we begin to reflect more deeply on each of the domains of the Integration Triad, we are developing our integrative identity. As we reflect on our views of integration, we always start from where we are, with the concrete reality of our lives, stories, life experiences. At any given moment, we are studying certain topics in psychology and not others, believing certain things about the world, culture, and politics and not others, speaking, understanding, and knowing God in certain ways and not other ways (Jinkins, 2015). While each of us may have some similarities in regard to our Christian faith (because of our belief in Jesus), we each bring something unique to the table in regard to our life experiences, family and cultural background, and interests in psychology. Thoughtful reflection on Christian theology, culture, and psychology usually helps develop our own integration views. In fact, Sandage and Brown (2018) insightfully observe that we are always doing psychology (making sense of human behavior) and theology (making sense of the transcendent things of the divine).

In this section, we'd like you to consider how developing our integrative view and identity is a process—a process that can lead to personal and spiritual transformation. The work of integrating culture, psychology, and the Christian faith is a place where we can experience and see the work of God in our life. In short, all thoughtful reflection on our cultural identities, psychology, and our Christian faith can be used by God to grow, shape, and develop us into who God wants us to be. In referring to the specific influence of our culture and theology, Kim-Kort (2012) states that the ongoing reflection on faith and culture is always "rooted in a posture toward the movement of the Holy Spirit, who seeks to connect and integrate and make whole" (p. 73). It is important to orient our hearts toward the movement of the Holy Spirit in this process, as practicing the work of integration can be a formative experience toward a more whole or integrated self (Kim-Kort, 2012). As we discuss how our integrative identities develop, ask the Holy Spirit to lead you to people who can help you understand your faith and cultural heritage more and ask God's Spirit to help you explore and reflect on your communities, contexts, and culture.

Theologian and minister Richard Rohr notes the importance of remembering that God is not absent from our day-to-day lives (Rohr, 1999). The truth is that we already exist and live in the presence of God, and what is often absent is our awareness of God's presence (Rohr, 1999). This simply means that as our integrative identities develop, it's valuable to keep in mind that God is already present with us. However, we continually need to foster an awareness of the work of God's Spirit as our integrative views and identities develop. James Martin, SJ, notes that slowing down and noticing the work of God in our life helps us realize that our life is already permeated and animated with the presence of God (Martin, 2012). Once you begin to slow down, notice, and look around, you will easily see the work of God in your life (Martin, 2012). Some experiences in life can be jarring, and they force us to reconsider our integrative views. Sometimes our integrative views are developed and transformed as we encounter God's blessings and experience joy and gratitude.

Thoughtful reflection between Christian theology, our cultural identity, and psychology is transformative because God's Spirit is involved in this process. If we are open to it, integrative reflection puts us in a position to listen and learn what God might be wanting to teach us about our faith, cultural identity, or even aspects of psychology. Our views of integration often develop as we have an experience in life that causes us to rethink assumptions about the world. When this occurs we can experience something thought-provoking (or even upsetting) in the way we see the world. Depending on what the experience of the situation is, we spend time trying to make sense and meaning of this new experience. This process of meaning-making develops our integrative identities, and in this chapter we discuss further how we make meaning of the various storylines of the Integration Triad.

The Cycle of Transformation:
Developing Our Integrative Identity

In our previous chapters, we have drawn your attention to the three domains of the Integration Triad, and have already given a more in-depth consideration to how you can begin to think and reflect more deeply about each one of these domains. Our views of integration are unique to each one of us and are shaped by our faith traditions, our cultural backgrounds, our understanding of key aspects of Scripture, and our own interests and knowledge of psychology. Each of us brings all our summative experiences of our lives, church background, understanding of God, and knowledge of psychology to the table when we practice integration. This is what makes the task of integration a rich and diverse experience.

Even with reflection on each of these domains of the Integration Triad, we also acknowledge that our views and beliefs are shaped and formed over time. Our consistent reflections and meaning-making experiences according to the Integration Triad begin to develop our integrative identity. *Our integrative identities develop as we get older, have different life experiences, and learn more about God, ourselves, our culture, and psychology.* These new life experiences or experiences of study and meaning-making force us to examine or rethink what we have previously known. While we all start where we are, we continue to be transformed through an iterative process of having new experiences and receiving new information which disrupts or challenges our normal way of thinking about God, our cultural identity, or psychology. This disruption or challenge results in more intentional reflection about our faith, cultural stories or psychology. This intentional reflection leads us to new ways of thinking, behaving, and believing—which is what helps develop our integrative identity. New ways of thinking, behaving, or believing provide us with a greater capacity to be integrated individuals and to work toward justice in our church, communities, and the wider society.

In conceptualizing the development of our integrative identity, we offer a diagram that represents the Cycle of Transformation. The Cycle of Transformation builds on Robert Brown and Michael Jinkins's concept of hermeneutics, and it is adapted here to apply to the integration between psychology and Christian theology (for further, see Brown, 1984; Jinkins, 2001). One of the adaptations we made to the diagram is that we imagine it existing as a spiral, in that achieving steps six and seven means growth that would be a foundation for even further development in response to the next precipitating event. As a result, developing our integrative identity is a process that we call the Cycle of Transformation, where we are continually learning new things about God, ourselves, and others from the standpoint of our faith, cultural identity, and studies in psychology, and these meaning-making experiences and reflections foster further growth and development that ultimately leads us to new ways of thinking, behaving, and believing.

Key Concept 5.2

Our integrative identities develop as we have experiences that cause us to rethink assumptions about the world and to reflect on Scripture, psychology, and our cultural identity in new ways.

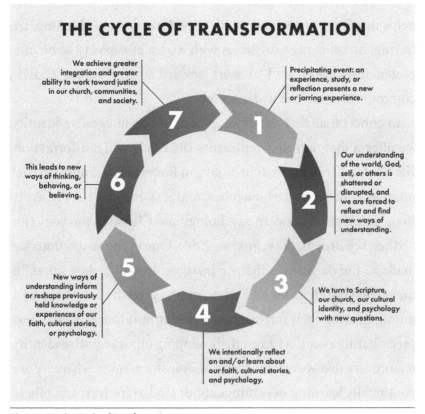

THE CYCLE OF TRANSFORMATION

1 — Precipitating event: an experience, study, or reflection presents a new or jarring experience.

2 — Our understanding of the world, God, self, or others is shattered or disrupted, and we are forced to reflect and find new ways of understanding.

3 — We turn to Scripture, our church, our cultural identity, and psychology with new questions.

4 — We intentionally reflect on and/or learn about our faith, cultural stories, and psychology.

5 — New ways of understanding inform or reshape previously held knowledge or experiences of our faith, cultural stories, or psychology.

6 — This leads to new ways of thinking, behaving, or believing.

7 — We achieve greater integration and greater ability to work toward justice in our church, communities, and society.

Figure 5.1. The Cycle of Transformation

Many times, a deeper consideration of our integrative reflections or beliefs is set in motion by a *precipitating event* (step 1), which ranges from an ordinary, day-to-day event to a jarring event. An example of a more ordinary event would be reading this book for a class assignment, and a jarring precipitating event would be experiencing racism, sexism, or even experiencing death of someone close to you, or being a victim of violence. An event that may fall in between these two extremes might be having tense conversations with friends or family members about differing perspectives on politics or emotionally charged world events. Or perhaps it is a topic within psychology that brings up a new question about your faith, a class that exposes you to new material that you are excited about, or maybe an experience of grief or loss that changes how you see the world without a key relationship or influence. The events that cause a jarring experience and develop our integrative identities can also be brought about by a personal and career milestone, like starting a new internship or job, getting married, or a birth in your family. Any of these may be precipitating events that trigger reflection on your faith, cultural identities, or maybe even an aspect of psychology. In what follows, we explore more how the Cycle of Transformation involves meaning-making, in addition to providing two examples of how our integrative identities develop through the Cycle of Transformation.

Meaning-making within integration. Tedeschi et al. (1998) have extensively studied growth that occurs after a crisis (called posttraumatic growth) and found that a component of a crisis is the disruption of core belief. When a core belief that we hold is dismantled, we often find ourselves in a crisis. Such core beliefs can include: "I will continue to live my life with relative health for the foreseeable future," or "my community and people like me can live safely in this country without targeted threats of being assaulted." When these core beliefs are disrupted, we often feel disoriented, and it takes time to process these complex thoughts and feelings (Tedeschi et al., 1998).

More recent contributions to meaning-making include the concepts of global meaning and appraisals of specific situations (Park, 2010; Steger & Park, 2012). Generally speaking, a person's global meaning is the framework that gives purpose to one's life, and can include beliefs about God, others, and oneself. However, whether we think of one's global meaning or core belief, it is true that stress, distress, or trauma occurs when there is an event that causes us to doubt, question, or rethink a core belief or global meaning that has given our life purpose (Steger & Park, 2012).

We as authors hold that a core piece of integration and developing our integrative identity is making-meaning of an event, belief, practice, or situation. That is, meaning-making occurs when there is a precipitating event that forces us to rethink aspects of God, self, or others (step 2). Crystal Park (2010) notes that meaning-making can happen on an automatic or unconscious level, or it can be more deliberate. We can think of what we are doing here in this book as being an attempt to be more deliberate about our meaning-making. Interestingly enough, Park (2010) also notes how people regularly use their communities and religious or spiritual beliefs to make sense out of loss, death, and struggle. This is displayed in our Cycle of Transformation under step three, where we draw on Scripture, church, cultural identities, and psychology to try to make sense of a situation.

Precipitating event: Grief and loss. One example of a precipitating event that often forces us to reflect and move toward greater understanding is the circumstance of grief, death, and loss. I (William) had been to many funerals in my church growing up, but never had someone really close to me pass away until I was in my early twenties. In college when I got the call during swim practice that I was to come home immediately because my grandfather only had a few more days to live, my understanding of grief, loss, and death changed in a new, painful, and different way. When I finally arrived at the hospital, I realized that my family was wrong. My grandfather didn't have a few days to live—he only had a few hours. As he was hooked into machines that beeped and hissed, we spent our last hours as a family saying goodbye, telling my grandfather that we loved him, and praying with him. I watched him die there in front of me, in the hospital surrounded by our family. Seeing his death in person profoundly shaped my views of grief—there's a deep loss, confusion, finality, and powerlessness to it all. Some of you who have seen someone die might be able to relate to how the person actually looks different once they pass away. That was the case with my grandfather. Although there were similarities in his physical appearance after he passed away compared to when he was alive, I remember being shocked at how he actually looked like a different person the instant the breath of his life had left him. As much as I wanted to do something, there was nothing that I could do. While I believe that God was there with him and our family, I still was angry that God could let this happen.

My physical and emotional relationship with my grandfather changed at that point, and it was only years later that I realized that even though his physical presence was gone, he continued to occupy an active place in my memory in a formative way. My relationship with him and memories of him continue to strengthen and inspire me. In this case, the initial death of my grandfather was the precipitating event of steps one and two in the Cycle of Transformation.

As we slowly move forward from hearing or witnessing a loss, our experiences in life regarding death deepen our knowledge of how we understand grief and loss, since they often force us to rethink categories of things that we have learned before (steps 3 and 4 on our Cycle of Transformation above). These personal experiences have potential to move us to more deliberative and intentional theological and integrative reflection—though at the time we might not know this.

Steps four, five, and six on the Cycle of Transformation happened for me when I began to realize (sometime much later) how my abstract knowledge of grief and loss had been informed and broadened by my own practical and lived experience of grief and loss. For example, before the experience of my grandfather's death, I had knowledge of death in a very abstract way, and this was changed when I went through the pain, grief, and loss of experiencing his death firsthand. As we stumble, study, pray, and reflect through these jarring life events, we are changed in the process. Sometimes this journey is dark, sometimes it involves pain and lament, sometimes it involves some sunlight and hope—but most often the experiences of our lives are a mixture of all of these. Nicholas Wolterstorff's classic work *Lament for a Son* speaks to this process of experiential encounter with grief and loss, and how it changes one's views and theology, better than any other book that I know of. In his deeply heartfelt, vulnerable, and wise style of writing, Wolterstorff describes the loss of his own son to a climbing accident, how he grieved the loss of his son, and how his view of life, God, the cross, and suffering changed forever because of it.

It wasn't until sometime later, however, that I was able to recognize how this experience of grief and loss enabled me to work toward justice in my particular context (steps 6 and 7 on the Cycle of Transformation). It was only after I began working in a church, and then working as a therapist that I began to see how I was able to stay present with those who had experienced death or loss, in a way that I wasn't able to before. Of course I did not know this at the time of my grandfather's death, but years later I was able to see how I approached those who were suffering with a different kind of openness and ability to stay present. Justice in this particular context looked like staying present and honoring the stories of those who shared their pain with me. Hearing about the pain of loss is powerful because if we listen well, we also hear about how a person was changed and impacted by the person they are grieving.

Precipitating event: Cultural awareness. Let's consider a hypothetical scenario as another example of how the Cycle of Transformation can occur. Imagine a college student, Jen, is having a conversation with her friend John after class one day. They are talking about the Black Lives Matter protests, and they have sharply different positions on this topic. This precipitating event left Jen feeling surprised because she and John usually agree on many things, including opinions, preferences, and even style. This difference in viewpoints may lead to Jen's initial reflection of her cultural stories (step 2), which in this case is asking the question of "Why do John and I think very differently on this?" This may lead to Jen noting superficial cultural differences, such as John is of Euro-American background, which is different from Jen's Asian American background, and Jen wonders if this is why they differ in perspectives. In this scenario, Jen's Asian American culture was a part of her social identity that had stayed in the background for the most part, but this precipitating event brought an awareness of this part of her that she does not usually think about. To take further steps toward greater integration, Jen might choose to intentionally reflect on her cultural stories (step 4) in the domain of ethnicity. This may include steps such as talking to family members about what this identity means to them. This may include stories of migration from countries of origin or what it is like for them to be Asian Americans, which at times also includes stories of discrimination (ChenFeng, 2018a). In this step, Jen may choose to understand this identity more outside of her family stories, for example by reading books on Asian American experiences,[2] or watching the PBS documentary series *Asian Americans*. She may also have intentional conversations with other Asian American friends to understand what it means for them to be Asian Americans. As you can see, this process may take place over a long period of time, and Jen may cycle through the steps several times without another precipitating event. In other words, Jen may go from one, two, three, four, five, six, back to three and so forth, as she is now committed to continually deepening her awareness of this identity. After step four, Jen finds herself having a deeper understanding, awareness, and appreciation of her Asian American heritage (step 5), including her family's history and larger Asian American communities. She may find a greater sense of pride for the resilience and strength in her family for enduring discrimination in their early years in the United States. She may find that she is able to draw on this legacy of resilience as she faces difficulty, such as reminding herself that she comes from a lineage of strong women who have endured much.

---

[2]For instance, Lee, E. (2015). *The making of Asian America: A history.* Simon & Schuster.

As Jen continues to learn specific cultural influences in her family, church, and community at large, she may find that there are values with which she does not agree. For example, Mihee Kim-Kort (2012) and Grace Ji-Sun Kim (Kim & Shaw, 2018) both write about how a part of their Asian American Christian heritage growing up was the assumption that women typically take roles in ministry that center around preparing food in the kitchen and other service roles. Jen may find that this, too, was a part of her family's story, but one that she moves away from as she re-shapes previously held knowledge or experiences of her faith, culture, and psychology (step 5), which is informed by her identity as a woman and a Christian. As a part of this process of intentional reflection and meaning-making, Jen finds herself more at home with the values and inheritances of her Asian identity, and also able to name values that she has chosen to differentiate from. In this way, she has grown her capacity to tell her stories in a greater constellation of identities (step 6), which makes hermeneutical resources further available to other Asian American Christian women as well (see chapter 6 on hermeneutical injustice). Her reflection and meaning-making also allow her to move toward extending love and greater justice toward herself and others in the Christian community (step 7), as she engages in ministry roles that are not limited to just preparing food but also include areas that steward her talents and gifts, such as leading Bible studies or other leadership roles.

Integration as a Spiritual Process over Time

As in the quote by Yo-Yo Ma at the beginning of this chapter, we must begin to recognize the embedded nature of our context and work to find our voices beyond those that have been assigned to us. Truly, our voices, our natural music and rhythm can never be separated from our faith, psychology, and cultural stories. Ultimately, a part of transformation is to engage in an ongoing process of critically evaluating these influences to find our own identities within. The work of integrating culture, psychology, and the Christian faith is a place where we can experience and see the work of God in our life. The Cycle of Transformation is simply one way to understand how our integrative identities are formed over time. All thoughtful reflection on our cultural identities, psychology, and Christian faith can be used by God to grow, shape, and develop us into who he wants us to be.

Psychology has shown that, while our models (psychosocial stages, moral development, hierarchy of needs, etc.) have been described in a linear manner in the past, in reality, growth is non-linear and requires the unique interaction of persons and context over time (Blozis, 2012; Roberts, 1986). In a similar way, our own Cycle of Transformation, developing our integrative views and identity, is a process that occurs over time. Here, we are just approaching our integrative identity development in a small window of time, maybe over the course of a semester or a year. More intentional reflection about your faith, psychology, and culture will continue to develop over your life as you more intentionally reflect on your faith and the discipline of psychology. The reality is that integrating our Christian faith, the discipline of psychology, and our cultural identities is ultimately done over the course of our lifetime.

As you can see in the examples above from William and the hypothetical situation from Jen, our integrative identity is formed over time, and it is one that can lead to personal and spiritual transformation. As we allow ourselves to be changed by God's

Spirit in this process, new ways of thinking, behaving, or believing take place. In the examples above, when Jen is able to be more at home with her Asian identity and name the values that she has chosen to differentiate from, she is able to think and believe differently about her cultural heritage. In the example that William gave above, as he recognized the ways that his grandfather had shaped his identity, he was able to move to new ways of thinking about death and loss. As he read the book *Lament for a Son*, he was also able to behave differently with those who were suffering.

However, it is important to remember that moving toward developing our integrative identity means that we should start by simply taking stock of where we are. While we hope this book isn't a jarring experience that causes additional stress in your life, we do hope that it might be part of steps one and two on the Cycle of Transformation that provides you with new thoughts or opportunities to reflect on past assumptions. As we develop our integrative identity, our faith informs this process because we remember that God's Spirit is ever present in this process of development and transformation. Dallas Willard, in his well-known book *The Divine Conspiracy*, reminds us that transformation is actually carried out in our real life "where we dwell with God and our neighbors" (Willard, 1998, p. 348). Willard notes that first, "we must accept the circumstances we constantly find ourselves in as the place of God's kingdom and blessing," since "God has yet to bless anyone except where they actually are" (Willard, 1998, p. 348).

As seen in the Cycle of Transformation, as we change, we move to greater ways to extend love and work toward justice (step 7). This new place of transformation in our identity is now our new starting place where we will begin again to develop our ideas even further (step 1) as we are confronted with a new experience, reflection, or a part of our studies that forces us to rethink previously held assumptions (steps 1-2-3).

Wrapping Things Up

We hope that by applying the Cycle of Transformation, you will move toward having a greater ability to bring about love and justice in your respective circles of influences. In speaking of the integration journey, J. Derek McNeil reminds us how this is connected to our identity being shaped and formed over time, and how this moves us to greater action and service.

> This heroic journey is not just about identity and self-discovery; it is also about service to a community. Consequently, while I believe that all integration is personal, it is also contextual/communal, happening in a historical space in which there are certain questions that we are all trying to answer and certain realities that we are all trying to live with. . . . This complex setting will raise a host of old and new questions, each of which must be engaged. You may feel reluctant, as I did, for fear that you do not have an adequate voice or do not have a part to play, but each generation always needs its heroes and heroines to say yes. Taking your heroic integration journey is more than just a philosophical exercise—it is to be used by God to do the thing you were born to do. (McNeil, 2010, pp. 207-8)

Our hope is that as a community, we would move toward the construction of an integrated world that is varied, imaginative, and honors cultural traditions and identities. Bringing diverse voices into integration is not a task that is ever fully finished; it is part of the task of working toward justice. As your own integrative identity is formed and transformed over time, you are helping create and contribute toward a more just vision of integration that honors, listens to, and respects cultural traditions, and that works to extend love and justice.

Reflection Questions

1. Describe a situation or jarring experience that impacted your life in the past. What was the event? Why was it difficult? Any event or experience is valid; it just has to be something that has impacted you.

2. How did this experience cause you to question aspects of your faith, something within psychology, and something within your culture?

3. Where did you turn for answers? Were these people or resources helpful? Why or why not?

4. Did you gain new forms of understanding your situation or experience? If so, how? If not, why?

5. In what new ways did you learn to view God or others through this experience? What new things did you learn about yourself or someone else? Did any of your studies in psychology help you understand your experience more? If so, how?

6. How did you integrate these new experiences or lessons into your life? How have you grown or changed as a result of this experience?

7. Step back for a moment to pause and reflect on your answers to the questions above. What thoughts, emotions, or bodily sensations are you experiencing? Be honest about whatever feelings you might be having. What might God be saying through these experiences of feelings even now?

Honoring Cultural and Communal Wisdom

Long before I had heard the phrase
"the integration of psychology and theology,"
the concept of trying to see life the way God
sees it was familiar to me. In fact, I have
never known a different way. Integration
is not something I learned during my
years in Christian higher education; rather,
those years in Christian higher education
taught me the labels and vocabulary for
something I had learned much earlier.

M. ELIZABETH LEWIS HALL (2010)

As I reflect on this, I realize that for my
parents, there was very little separation
between what it meant to be a Christian and
what it meant to be personally and socially
accountable. . . . One's personal faith has
social and global consequences. . . .
Holiness promotes justice.

J. DEREK MCNEIL (2010)

In our last chapter, we discussed how our integrative identity develops through the Cycle of Transformation. This often occurs through a precipitating event that causes (or forces) us to more intentionally reflect on God, culture, and psychology which can lead us to a deeper awareness and understanding of the same. As we mentioned in our last chapter, this deepened understanding of God, cultural identity, and psychology produces changes in thoughts and behavior—one of those being a greater capacity to love others and work toward justice in our church, communities, and wider society.[1]

In this chapter, we'd like to broaden some of the ways we work toward greater love and justice by demonstrating how, as Christians practicing psychology, we can address injustices that may have occurred within the integrative dialogue between psychology and the Christian faith. In short, working toward greater love and justice in our church, communities, and society begins by addressing past injustices in our particular embodied contexts and recovering silenced parts of our own identities. In this chapter, we argue that (1) working toward greater love and justice involves honoring both the contextualized integrative stories that have been handed to us and the diverse cultural stories of integration, and (2) theological reflection from different cultural contexts provides rich resources for integration and can deepen and broaden the integration dialogue. As authors, our hope is to empower you as students to dive deeper into your own cultural identities. We also hope that by doing so, there will be more diverse voices at the table of integrating psychology and Christian theology.

---

[1]Portions of this chapter have also appeared in Dwiwardani & Whitney (2022) and Whitney et al. (2023).

Hermeneutical Injustice and Integration

For some time now, Christians doing interdisciplinary work between psychology and the Christian faith have felt the need for a more diverse approach to Christian integration (see Sandage & Brown, 2018; Strawn et al., 2018), but progress toward this has often been slow (Shelton & Dwiwardani, 2022). In fact, the integration literature has not always represented the diverse voices and cultures that make up the integration community (Shelton & Dwiwardani, 2022). This is an example of what Miranda Fricker (2007) calls epistemic injustice. According to her, there are two kinds of epistemic injustice: testimonial injustice and hermeneutical injustice (Fricker, 2007).

Testimonial injustice is ascribing less credibility to someone because of their social identity (gender, ethnicity, race, etc.), such as when someone is not believed by the police because that person is Black (Fricker, 2007), or when medical professionals believe a nurse report over an elderly patient's own report due to stereotypes of elderly patients having memory deficits (Carel & Kidd, 2014). These testimonial injustices are examples of assumptions made because of stereotypes and demographics (in this case, the Black person who was not believed, and the elderly patient whose direct report was not believed), specifically about their capacities to give accurate testimonies of what they know or experienced. In fact, testimonial injustice occurs anytime the person telling their story is silenced (intentionally or not), not heard, or not believed because of the privilege, bias, or prejudice of the one hearing the story (Fricker, 2007). Hermeneutical injustice, on the other hand, occurs "when a gap in collective interpretive resources puts someone at an unfair disadvantage when it comes to making sense of their social experiences" (Fricker, 2007, p. 1). In this chapter, we will focus on hermeneutical injustice as it applies to the integration of psychology and Christian faith. An extended treatment of whether testimonial injustice also takes place in the field of integration is a worthy endeavor; however, it is beyond the scope of this chapter.

Fricker (2007) states that understanding our experiences, along with sharing our knowledge, are basic to who we are as knowers. Having resources to make sense of our stories in our various social identities is a type of privilege. For example, US history books have not justly represented Native American, Black American, Latine American,[2] and Asian American stories (see An, 2020; Padgett, 2015; Unidos US & John Hopkins School of Education, 2023; Wolf, 1992, among others). As a result, many who identify with these racial groups do not have access to as many resources in making sense of their own and their ancestors' stories and experiences in literature compared to those who identify as White. Women who are in the fields of science, technology, engineering, and mathematics (STEM) find themselves in a male-dominated space, and their experiences as women in these fields are not as widely represented in the literature as men's. While this is beginning to change, there are hermeneutical injustices when it comes to making sense of one's own experiences as a woman in STEM due to having access to fewer stories and representations.

---

[2] The term *Latine* represents a recent development in the literature; it is gender inclusive and a term that fits more naturally into the Spanish language, as compared to *Latinx* (Kamara, 2021). In reviewing recent scholarly literature, there has been an increase in the use of the term *Latine*, and the authors chose this term for the book, while recognizing that there is a diversity of opinions in continuing dialogue on the topic.

Key Concept 6.1

Hermeneutical injustice occurs when someone is at a disadvantage in making sense of their history or experience because of a lack of interpretive resources.

As you think of your cultural stories and the Cycle of Transformation, there may be areas of your social identity that are more difficult to make sense of than others. One possible reason is that the stories predominantly written about and shared are not your stories, and as a result, you may not have access to as large a reservoir of language and resources with which to make sense of these stories. Some social identities have been privileged to tell their stories in a public way—predominating the literature with just one perspective and constituting a kind of power. On a related note, this idea is highlighted by author Chimamanda Adichie (2009) in her TED talk "The Danger of a Single Story," which we would encourage you to pause here and watch.

Testimonial and hermeneutical injustice in the church. In his book *Is Christianity the White Man's Religion? How the Bible Is Good News for People of Color*, Antipas Harris (2020) describes how minority voices have been marginalized in the church when understanding and interpreting the Bible. Harris asserts that the dominant framework in training ministers has privileged mostly male and Eurocentric perspectives, and often these male and Eurocentric voices have used the Bible to justify slavery, oppression, and segregation (Harris, 2020). Harris is not dismissing White male contributions, nor is he only privileging Black voices in interpreting the Bible. However, Harris's main argument is that it is important for us to have diverse perspectives when interpreting the Bible. To put his critique into context, other theologians of color have been reminding us of this for a while now (e.g., see Bacote, 2020; J. Cone, 2012). For instance, Harris states:

> An oppressive past follows us, albeit its form has been modified as not to appear overt. Consider how oppression comes in so many forms. For example, the way theology and biblical studies are taught in the church and the academy advantage eighteenth- and nineteenth-century Western ways of thinking over other diverse ways of thinking. By doing so, the schools sustain colonial superstructures that marginalize the hard work African American and other ethnic or racial minority scholars have done to advance new insights into a God who privileges underprivileged people by placing them on an equal playing field with all others. As a result of colonization in the shaping of the Christian mind, legalized, passive oppression continues by silencing voices in the church. (Harris, 2020, p. 70)

When we have individuals whose voices are not heard or represented, there is an injustice that is taking place. Unfortunately, our churches (and integration communities and literature) silence certain identities and stories by privileging other majority culture voices and stories. We acknowledge that this is often done unintentionally, but that unintentionally is often the problem—that is, it happens unconsciously without people even knowing that hermeneutical injustice is taking place. Consequently, to practice integration without considering culture and context is to perpetuate hermeneutical injustice.

A part of what contributes to the problem is that much of the integration literature has been written by academics. In academia and institutional leadership, the number of women and people of color represented are not proportionate to the student body or population at large (Menges & Exum, 1983; Ware, 2000). This is another reason that only looking in the academy for embodied examples of integration presents a significant challenge, since students often do not see their own traditions, cultures, or gender represented among their mentors and academic role models when learning integration. This is a problem that needs to be systematically addressed in academia, but also among those of us who are teaching courses on integration.

When there are individuals whose voices are not heard or represented, even if this is unintentional, hermeneutical injustice is taking place. Moreover, when we do not actively engage culture and identities, many students of integration who in fact have much to contribute to the literature may find themselves at a disadvantage of language and resources with which to make sense of their integration stories. To name this hermeneutical injustice is an important and urgent task if we are to respond to the call of greater diversity in the integration literature. As we give voice to our own experiences that have historically been marginalized, we become witnesses to the ways that God has intricately been present in our varying experiences. As such, we move toward "a fresh space to live into and out of God's whole redemption" (Kim-Kort, 2012, p. xiii). In reclaiming parts of ourselves that have historically been unnamed, we are paying attention to a fuller picture of God's creative and generative work in our lives, and in doing so, our own transformation becomes a vehicle toward bringing greater justice to others (Kim & Shaw, 2018).

Becoming conduits of love and justice by doing the work in our lives. As we give voice to different parts of ourselves that have historically been marginalized and choose to humbly listen to others, we become witnesses to the ways that God has intricately been present in the varying experiences of our lives and the lives of others around us. As we discover parts of our own lives that have been silenced, it is important to speak out of these silenced identities. Though parts of our lives may have been silenced due to hermeneutical injustice, God's work in these areas is just as important as that in your more privileged identities, in which your stories have been freely shared. In reclaiming these parts of ourselves, we are paying attention to a fuller picture of God's creative and generative work in our lives, and in doing so, our own transformation helps us extend love and work toward justice in helping others listen to and speak about the multiple facets of their own identities (Kim & Shaw, 2018).

Uncovering our silenced cultural stories is both a crucial and urgent task. Since our history or theology excludes the historically marginalized voices, we miss out on seeing the depths of God's diversity and work within our complex, multidimensional lives. Moreover, the exclusion of nondominant voices from the integration conversation perpetuates hermeneutical injustice by overlooking those who are made in God's image. Just as hermeneutical injustice has taken place in the training of Christian ministers and the church (Carter, 2008; Harris, 2020), interpretive lenses in the integration literature have often left many voices marginalized and important questions unasked.

Ultimately, we engage in the reflections of our history and identity in order to become transformed by God's Spirit. As we enter into a more complete understanding of God's redemption of our lives, we become aware of the ways that Christ has been present in our histories and our identities (even ones that have been relatively more silenced). As discussed, God's Spirit has been actively shaping our lives and stories in all of our multifaceted experiences. Knowing and reflecting on how God has been working and shaping our rich and multifaceted experiences actually helps us grow in a deeper intimacy with Christ. Further, reclaiming parts of ourselves that have sunk below the surface presents an opportunity to bring them to God for healing and transformation, and to be conduits of healing in this world.

Working toward greater love and justice through intentional awareness. We believe that Christ has been at work in our lives from before we were born and in ways that we may not even be aware of. As we engage in an intentional process of reflecting on our stories from areas that might have been silenced in the past, we allow God's redemptive and restorative justice to take place. Some areas in your life may make you feel very "at home," such as your ethnicity or gender. You may know your cultural stories in these areas very well and have many resources by which you are able to make sense of your experiences in these areas. Some other cultural identities may be areas that feel a bit more hazy or confusing for you because these stories have not been readily understood, given the hermeneutical resources available to you. Said another way, you may have found yourself experiencing hermeneutical injustices in not having resources to make sense of your own story. As we mentioned in chapter two, an important step is to recognize that God is not absent from this process of reflection on any part of the storylines within the Integration Triad. Deeper reflection on culture and on hermeneutical and testimonial injustices is not only important for us to become more integrated persons, but it is an important way that we open up parts of our lives to God's Spirit for healing. As you bring some of these unfamiliar or unseen parts of your cultural story to light, you become more integrated as a person. In the Cycle of Transformation, deeper reflection in steps one through six leads us to be able to work toward greater justice in our church, communities, and wider society.

Key Concept 6.2

As we reclaim the silenced parts of ourselves, we are changed in the process and become conduits of healing and justice in our churches, communities, and wider societies.

Love and justice through contextual differentiation. We have spent much of this chapter and chapter four discussing the importance of naming, honoring, uncovering the cultural influences in which we are embedded. Honoring and naming our own cultural stories are ways that we can extend love to our family and cultural history by noticing the ways that God has been working in our family and culture. The value in these reflections is that we can begin to notice the ways in which God has intricately designed the influences that shaped us that extend far beyond our current locality and time in history.

However, we need to make an important point here. While cultural tradition, heritage, and influence should be honored, they do not dictate us. In fact, as we dive deep into our heritages, we might (and often do) find customs and values that are not in line with what Scripture teaches. This is where the work of restorative justice needs to take place. As we reflect on our cultural identities, we also might find teachings or values that go against some of the best practices in current psychological research. This is another place where restoration might need to occur.

For example, when my (Carissa's) grandmother converted to Christianity in her adult years, she had long been practicing animism with fervent devotion. She shared stories of leaving offerings in front of her bedroom every night before bedtime to ward off evil spirits. There was also a family heirloom that had been passed down from generation to generation that was believed to be a representation of the spiritual realm. This heirloom was an object called "keris" (a type of asymmetrical dagger). It was believed that this keris brought our family good fortune and safety from danger. Before our family's introduction to Christianity, orienting their lives around the spiritual realm was already embodied and practiced for many generations. Specifically, my family held a deeply embedded and practiced belief that safety and provision are divine blessings.

When my grandmother converted to Christianity, she gave up her keris and devoted her entire life to Christ. Although devotion to the keris was arguably an important part of our family's heritage and culture, it was incompatible with my grandmother's faith in Jesus. This was an example of how developing in integration may include differentiating from some aspects of our cultural background. However, it may also mean integrating some other aspects of our cultural backgrounds. In my grandmother's case, she continued to practice the same devotion and oriented her life completely around her newfound faith. While she undoubtedly had much to learn in her Christian faith, the integration of spirituality into her daily life was already a practiced rhythm and orientation. Having seen how she lived her life, I know that the unquestioned view of safety and provision as God's gifts also moved her toward generosity. She was generous and hospitable because she believed deeply that all that she had was a gift from God. In the same way that God is the God of our story even before we enter into a relationship with him, God was the God of my family's story. My grandmother's devotion to her spiritual life served as a background to her Christian life, which became part of my story as well. Growing up, I observed and was impacted by how integrated the Christian faith was for my grandmother: in her generosity, in her decision-making, in the way she prayed and read the Bible every morning and night, and in the way she taught me how to pray about everything, even the small things in life.

As we are encouraging you to reflect on your own cultural heritages, you may begin to uncover aspects of them that might not align with Christianity. Or, as you reflect on your cultural stories, you might find that part of your cultural heritage is a legacy of White supremacy or other forms of racism. And at times, as you reflect on your theological beliefs, you may find that they are not consistent with psychological science. The concept of differentiation first came out of the literature on family therapy, and is defined as "the ability to identify one's own thoughts and feelings separately from that of the family" (ChenFeng, 2018a, p. 16). As you reflect on the heritages and cultures of your family, localities, and ADDRESSING communities, it is important to identify your own thoughts and feelings in relation to them. This process, of both recognizing your influences and honoring them, and at the same time identifying your own thoughts and feelings in relation to them, is an ongoing process that reflects a journey toward maturity. This is called *contextual differentiation* (ChenFeng, 2018a, 2018b), defined as "identifying one's own thoughts and feelings as they are influenced by, related to, or different from one's context" (p. 17), and it is part of what is described in our Cycle of Transformation discussion under numbers two, three, and four. Since this is all a part of developing our integrative identity, we would go further to say that contextual differentiation for the Christian involves seeking the leading of the Holy Spirit. So, in this process, it is important to pause and reflect on the following insightful questions that Hyejin Shim (2017) poses, "What are the legacies we've inherited, which ones will we choose to protect, and which will we dismantle?" (para. 3).

Cultural stories of integration among historically marginalized communities. We believe that diverse cultural and theological perspectives at the table of integration enrich our integration efforts. In order for us to move toward this, we have to remember that the role of community is crucial for us to begin to hear diverse voices. Given the challenges of uncovering our cultural stories (naming hermeneutical injustice and the water we swim in), existing with others in community is key in constructing a more varied integration. As Neff and McMinn (2020) note, integration happens as we begin to encounter one another through conversation. In a similar way, the process of unearthing our cultural inheritances in integration is best done as a communal and conversational process. As fish who are swimming in our own waters (Lee, 2022), we may discover language that helps us make sense of our own waters when we dialogue with one another. As we hear others' cultural stories, we are reminded of similar stories, and we become aware of contrasts. When we articulate our stories to an interested and empathic listener, we might also uncover stories and experiences that we have not thought of in a long time. Kim-Kort (2012) states that to "make oneself literally a person of integrity, a whole person, means openness and engagement. . . . It results in an intentional incorporation of other cultures with the attitude that they will help us understand our own stories even amidst conflict and differences" (p. 73). It is important to note that a part of this conversation and communal process is to realize values and priorities in the other person that you might disagree with, which is a crucial part of the process. A part of maturity is to tolerate differences without trying to change ourselves or the other person (Sandage & Brown, 2018; Sandage & Harden, 2011).

 Key Concept 6.3

Theological perspectives from BIPOC inform and broaden the integration between psychology and Christianity.

Since the mid-1960s and 1970s the discipline of Christian theology has cataloged a broad array of ways that the Christian faith is integrated into various cultures and communities (Antonio, 2011; Flemming, 2005). Take, for example, the way that various cultural communities have coped with trauma, stressors, and chronic illnesses (Bryant-Davis et al., 2013). Much of this interface between one's localized context and Christian theology has not shown up on the radar of more academic pursuits of integration between psychology and Christianity. However, it draws on embodied

Christian theological wisdom and represents a rich, embodied integration that goes back centuries (prior to the existence of more formalized academic approaches to the integration of psychology and Christianity).

By learning the ways that communities of color have integrated psychology and faith, we find a richness and depth that unfortunately has been minimally represented in the integration literature to date (Shelton & Dwiwardani, 2022). Comas-Díaz (2016) asserts the importance of recognizing "the centrality of Spirit among communities of color" (p. 153). As we look toward more diverse voices in the integration literature, it is important to acknowledge that an embodied integration already exists within many communities of color. In this next section, we present four particular examples of academic scholarship that note the integral role of Christian theology in the psychological experiences of communities of color. We have chosen to focus on literature that highlights salient and relevant themes among Native Americans, Blacks, Latines, and Asians/Asian Americans. It is important to note, however, that the examples we included below are but examples; they do not represent the totality of the group experiences, given vast intragroup differences and considering that race is one dimension of many in people's experiences and identities. The main point we hope to convey is that communities of color have embodied aspects of Christian theology in a variety of ways not frequently represented in the academic integration literature, not that these are representative of the ways in which the communities practice or embody integration.

Native Americans. Richard Twiss (2015) writes, "There is only one Creator of heaven and earth. There are not 'many' Creators.

Just one! *All* of human and nonhuman creation comes from the Creator. There is not a Creator who created Africa and Africans, or Asia and Asians, or Europe and Europeans, and so forth" (p. 17). Moreover, the Creator is revealed in general revelation through cultures and creation (Twiss, 2015). Unfortunately, centuries of oppression have often left little space for the authentic expression of Native Americans in the church (see Twiss, 2015, for a more thorough description of the impact of Western hegemony on Native American Christian communities). In his book, Twiss highlights that there is often skepticism when it comes to accepting cultural expressions of worship that are nondominant.

Twiss (2015) discusses many areas in which Indigenous North American Christians are reclaiming their cultural identities so that the gospel is expressed in ways that are more fully authentic to the communities. Twiss (2015) argues Native American communities embrace the sacred in their day-to-day lives. This is in contrast to a Western system of knowledge which divorces the cognitive from the embodied and the sacred from the secular (Twiss, 2015). Furthermore, knowledge is understood as not just a body of listed doctrines that remain static. Rather, knowledge is relational (both with the divine and with one another; Twiss, 2015). As such:

> Theologizing is a living relational system; it's a communal enterprise. I want to suggest that if we view theology as a living conversation— the intersection of human and divine exchange, an invitation to community, or a dialogic connecting point in creation between heaven and earth—we begin to rescue Western theology from rational enterprise and hegemony and set into motion a free-from,

organic conversation between Creator and human and nonhuman creation. (p. 237)

Knowledge, in the biblical perspective, can refer to intellectual understanding of something, but most often when the Hebrew word is used, it refers to a relational knowledge (Achtemeier & Boraas, 1996) that depends on a personal relationship or personal experience (Genesis 4:1; 22:12). In English, the word *know* or *knowledge* most often refers to the intellectual apprehension of facts or ideas. In this way, the English-speaking word often lacks the depth of understanding in the true biblical sense of knowledge.

Overall, the priority of relational knowledge and the interpenetration of sacred and secular realms have been present in Indigenous North American communities for centuries, and exemplify one aspect of Indigenous North American culture that overlaps with biblical conceptions of knowledge and the connection between human and divine realms (Woodley, 2008). This represents an example of how Native American Christians actively engage their cultural heritage, and in doing so further enrich the integration dialogue and literature. What would integration look like, for instance, if we begin with an assumption of an intimate, communal knowledge of God and of one another? What are we missing in our integration journey if we only privilege cognitive or propositional theological knowledge as the starting point of integration?

Black Americans/African Americans. Compared to the rest of the American population, Black Americans are most likely to identify as Christians (79%; Pew Research Center, 2018, February). This is contrasted to Christian identification in the general

American population (71%), among Whites (70%), Latines (77%), and Asians (34%; Pew Research Center, 2018, April). Black Americans are also more likely to be religious than Whites and Latines. Black Americans are more likely to endorse a belief in God with absolute certainty (83%), agree that religion is very important in their lives (75%), pray daily (73%), and attend religious services at least once weekly (47%; Pew Research Center, 2018, April). As borne out by these statistics, the import of spirituality in Black lives goes back centuries, and it has remained firmly rooted even through centuries of discrimination, oppression, and injustice.

There is much we can learn from the theological reflection of Black Christian communities. Particularly, the spirituality of Black communities has aided in the search for meaning amid suffering. James H. Cone (2011), in his book *The Cross and the Lynching Tree*, states:

> Black faith emerged out of Black people's wrestling with suffering, the struggle to make sense out of their senseless situation, as they related their own predicament to similar stories in the Bible. On the one hand, faith spoke to their suffering, making it bearable, while, on the other hand, suffering contradicted their faith, making it unbearable. That is the profound paradox inherent in black faith, the dialectic of doubt and trust in the search for meaning, as blacks "walk[ed] through the valley of the shadow of death." (Ps 23:4; chapter 5, pp. 124-25)

In the field of psychology, especially in counseling and psychotherapy, students of psychology are constantly challenged to make sense of suffering. In Cone's description of a "profound paradox," there is a depth of wisdom that has been informed by generations of wrestling with the tension between having hope and coping with the reality of suffering.

One way this dialectic of hope and suffering informs sermons and music in Black churches is in what Banks and Lee (2016) call prophetic preaching. It is a practice of naming the brokenness of this world (systemic racism, injustices, etc.) while empowering the church to move toward the future reality of God's kingdom both in this world and beyond (Banks & Lee, 2016). The hand-in-hand naming of current realities (which in turn, validate experience) while providing empowerment supports individuals' psychological health and movement toward social justice at large (Banks & Lee, 2016; Bryant-Davis, 2020). Banks and Lee (2016) also describe a program called "Inspirational Singing," designed for homeless women which incorporate spiritual practices, such as spiritual singing, sharing of testimonies, and relationship building, among others. By incorporating these spiritual practices, the program provides validation, support, nurturing, and healing of the women's psychological health, with a sense of hope and empowerment (Banks & Lee, 2016).

As we listen to these insights from Black theology and spirituality, we find some important themes that can and should shape our integration efforts between psychology and Christianity. First, God stands in solidarity with those who are suffering and with those who have experienced racism or oppression (Cone, 2012a). This message can often be missed by those in positions of privilege who have not experienced racism, slavery, or racial oppression (Callaway & Whitney, 2022). In short, each of us must answer the question: How does the reality of God standing with those who are marginalized or oppressed redirect our research or practice within psychology?

Second, Black theologies remind us that one's faith and spirituality is never something abstract or disembodied. The wisdom and thought of leaders like James Cone speak to the importance of one's theology making a difference in the actual lived experience of others within the world. For instance, Cone (1970) notes that Christian theology "is never just a rational study of the being of God. Rather, it is a study of God's liberating activity in the world" (Cone, 1970, p. 1). In short, a study of God involves God's action within the world. Or, as Howard Thurman notes in *Jesus and the Disinherited*:

> The basic fact is that Christianity as it was born in the mind of this Jewish teacher and thinker appears as a technique of survival for the oppressed. . . . "In him was life; and this life was the light of men." Wherever his spirit appears, the oppressed gather fresh courage; for he announced the good news that fear, hypocrisy, and hatred, the three hounds of hell that track the trail of the disinherited, need have no dominion over them. (Thurman, 1996, p. 17)

Third, naming the brokenness found within the world due to racism and orienting one's vision toward justice has been pivotal for Black Christians in America. For instance, Womanist theologies (Christian theology by Black women) challenge the Christian church to use principles of justice to combat racism, while also drawing on the spiritual and moral wisdom passed down by grandmothers and mothers (Abernethy et al., 2006; Williams, 2012). One's spiritual community and connection with others are essential strengths within the Black community—as opposed to an individualistic focus often found in White Western expressions of theology and psychology (Armstrong et al., 2002).

The legacy of Martin Luther King Jr. stands prominently here as we remember that his vision of justice was shaped by his Christian theology and an understanding of God's love. According to King (1963), any human law that does not square with the moral law of God is unjust. Racism is unjust because it involves the diminishment and oppression of humanity based on race, and this does not align with God's law of love that upholds the dignity and value of humans, regardless of race (King, 2019). As King aptly noted in his famous *Letter from Birmingham Jail*: "Injustice anywhere is a threat to justice everywhere" (King, 1963, p. 3). *Letter from Birmingham Jail* is King's response to an open letter published by clergy that called his direct actions for civil rights "unwise and untimely" (King, 1963). However, for King, justice always involves both love and action (specifically nonviolent action) that speaks out, takes a stand against injustices, and actively works toward creating a more just society. What would Christianity-psychology integration look like when shaped by a Christian theological vision of justice, and the desire to prophetically name the realities of injustice, racism, and hope that occur within the Christian church and within the field of psychology?

Latine Americans. According to the Pew Research Center (2015), Latines are more likely to attend religious services regularly (39%) and endorse the importance of religion in their lives (59%) than the general American population (36% and 53%, respectively), with 48% of Latines reporting their religions as Roman Catholics and 25% Protestant (Pew Research Center, n.d.). Spirituality and religiosity, specifically Christianity, has been highlighted in the literature to be central to Latine culture and lives (Garzon & Tan, 1992). One of the themes that has been highlighted in the literature is the depth of meaning that faith and spirituality provides amid suffering, particularly in Catholicism (Garzon & Tan, 1992). The spiritual discipline of Lent and history of saints who have become martyrs underscore the meaning of suffering (Bach-y Rita, 1982, as cited in Garzon & Tan, 1992). In referring to the experiences of Latines, Isasi-Diaz (1996) states, "The *palabra de Dios* . . . refers to the unflinching belief that God is with us in our daily struggles" (p. 158). In suffering, the immanent presence of the Lord becomes a source of both meaning and strength.

For many Latines, spiritual practices are often the basis for seeing the world, coping with stressors, and finding healing. In other words, there is an integration of the "sacred with the secular" (Comas-Díaz, 2016, p. 152). Latines throughout history have drawn on deep spirituality in coping with stressors, fostering empowerment within the self and others, and connecting with community (and ancestry), social activism, and social justice (Comas-Díaz, 2016). Theologians such as María Pilar Aquino, Daisy Machado, and Jeanette Rodríguez describe the experience of *conquista* and *reconquista*, one of colonization and domination, where women and men are seen as aliens on their own land and are viewed as a "border crosser" (Aquino et al., 2002). This perspective of being in between two worlds means that there is a constant interpretation that has to occur between the dominant culture and the Latine community (Aquino et al., 2002). Moreover, Latine theologians note that Latines are not foreigners to the United States (as is often assumed by White majority culture in the United States) but are in fact an integral part of the history of the Americas (Martell-Otero et al., 2013). Aquino (1993) also points out that women have not been silent in Latin America throughout history, and, while their voices have often been omitted in the writing of history, there have been consistent exemplars of women over the centuries that have resisted, stood up, and spoken out for their communities and families in the face of oppression.

The integral nature of faith in the well-being of Latines has been documented in research as well. Moreno and Cardemil (2018) conducted interviews with forty Latines of Mexican origins (half the participants were Mexican-born, and half were US-born) and found that 65% of them endorsed that religiosity is crucial to their well-being. First, they identified social support as an important component of their religious lives (Moreno & Cardemil, 2018). Belonging to a faith community is a protective factor, especially for those who emigrated from Mexico and do not have family in the United States (Moreno & Cardemil, 2018). Second, when giving up control over their stressors to God, many experienced improvements in their sense of well-being (Moreno & Cardemil, 2018). Finally, almost half of the participants stated that their faith-based moral guidelines have kept them from stressors, such as ones that result from substance abuse and sexual promiscuity (Moreno & Cardemil, 2018). Among the many important findings in this study, Moreno and Cardemil (2018) found that Mexican-born immigrants tend to endorse higher religiosity (88%) than US-born Mexican Americans (37%). Moreno and Cardemil (2018) attribute this partly to the US-born participants' acculturating to a more individualized culture in the United States, thereby reducing the felt need for social connectedness in religious communities. What would integration look like if we actively seek to learn how Christian communities have been coping with stressors in ways that are supported by a larger culture of social connectedness?

How can the psychology-theology dialogues be enriched by centering the experiences of immigrants and refugees who may have lost this larger social connectedness as a support for their faith?

Asian/Asian Americans. Among evangelical Protestants, Asian Americans are more likely to attend weekly religious service (76%) than their White counterparts (64%; Pew Research Center, 2013). More Asian American Catholics (60%) attend religious service at least weekly, compared to White Catholics (47%; Pew Research Center, 2013). In addition, more Asian Americans (37%) state that living a very religious life is one of their most important goals compared to the general US adult (24%; Pew Research Center, 2013). Given the heterogeneity within the Asian/Asian American population, caution is important when making broad statements about the role of spirituality and religiosity in this group. However, the Pew Research Center (2013) data indicate that at least among Christians, Asian Americans seem to have a higher level of religious commitments on several indicators compared to the general US population. In speaking to the heterogeneity of religiosity and spirituality, Siang-Yang Tan (1991) notes that while traditional Asian beliefs of "multiple gods, goddesses, and spirits is theologically incompatible with the monotheism of Christianity, these traditional beliefs do translate readily into a Christian worldview that incorporates the existence of the supernatural realm" (as cited in Tan & Dong, 2014, p. 429). In other words, when Asians convert to Christian faith from other spiritual traditions, they often bring a way of living or interacting with the supernatural world that has been practiced in their families for generations.

One theme that is found across North American Asian women's theologies is the need to raise awareness of the particular type of experiences that these women face with regard to sexism and racism. Asian American theologies alert us to how these experiences are different depending on moments of immigration, ranging from first-generation Asian immigrants, to the 1.5 generation (born abroad but raised in America), to American-born Asian Americans (Tan, 2008). In the American context, being Asian/ Asian American often brings with it an experience of in-betweenness. Existing in these in-between spaces highlights a sense of disparateness and provides a unique opportunity to invite the Holy Spirit into bringing greater integration to one's life (Kim-Kort, 2012).

Challenges to the category of Asian are part of this discourse, since the label "Asian" or "Asian American" is far too simplistic, as Nami Kim (2007) notes. For instance, Nami Kim describes her experience of immigration as one who came as a foreign visitor from Asia to the United States, becoming a resident Korean within the United States, and now identifies as part of the Asian North American community (Kim, 2007). This progression of her experience and existing in these in-between spaces—being an outsider within the US context—is an experience that is commonly spoken of in North American Asian theologies (Kim, 2007). Full dignity of personhood is diminished when Asian American women or men are stereotypically viewed as the model immigrant while also being seen as perpetually foreign and never fully assimilated as an American (Yee, 2007).

Kim-Kort (2012) writes of the intertwining of Asian/Asian American women's experiences and Christian theology. While she is not explicitly drawing a connection with psychology as an academic discipline, many of the experiences she writes about are important psychological processes, such as identity, decision-making, and emotions (Kim-Kort, 2012). For example, when it comes to racial relations, Asian Americans often find themselves in between race narratives which usually revolve around Black and White relations. She elaborates, "African-American communities would often identify Asian Americans with European Americans, while Asian Americans are often relegated to some ambiguous minority status by the dominant culture" (p. 4). Asians/Asian Americans often find it difficult to place themselves in the race relations conversation, while at the same time having experiences that are relevant to the conversation. This often impacts the formation of identity as it relates to society.

Further, specifically in addressing identity formation among women: Asian American women are compelled to constantly take into consideration the surrounding dominant culture and expectations of non-Asian men and women. The complicated structure of these relationships often acts as a further barrier to these women when it comes to identity development in the home, in the church, in the political arena, or in the workplace (Kim-Kort, 2012, p. 21). In this way, Asian/Asian American women, in making sense of their racialized and gendered experiences, often note the limited resources to make sense of their narratives. The pressures of having to consider the dominant US culture and expectations of non-Asian men and women often become a barrier to developing one's identity in various arenas (Kim-Kort, 2012). The centrality of Christian theology in navigating through these challenges is clear as she describes a type of spirituality that is birthed out of Asian women's experiences.

Kim-Kort (2012) argues that the Holy Spirit is intimately involved in these lived experiences of Asian American women, and in relying on the Spirit, Asian/Asian American women can draw on these disparate experiences to become more integrated and empowered to bring about change and justice in our surroundings. She states, "It is the Holy Spirit, working through the disruptive nature of the confrontation between the center and periphery of these communities, who helps us discover a better understanding of all of our life stories" (Kim-Kort, 2012, p. 78). Thus, the lived experience of being a part of the church community enables healing to occur on individual and communal levels. What would the Christianity-psychology integration literature look like if we learn from traditions that more actively engage the Holy Spirit's presence in our day-to-day life? What would integration look like if we actively take into account the way the Holy Spirit is present in the in-between experiences of our communities?

Restorative Justice in Integration

The above are but some examples of literature that acknowledges the ways contextual experiences and contextual Christian theologies can inform everyday psychological experiences (the way we cope, the way we form identity, etc.). There is so much more on these lines of thinking (each is a whole literature in and of itself), and we are far from having represented each of them in any sufficiency. What we hope to have conveyed is the reality that before the term "integration of Christianity and psychology" was coined, there were many examples of how contextualized Christian theological reflections impacted psychological well-being. As a result, many communities of color have a lived and embodied theology that is practical, rooted in one's lived experience, and oriented toward action within the world and between other fellow humans.

In striving toward diversity in integration, we show love by learning from rich traditions and expanding the table of integration to include these voices. Only in doing so can we truly expand and enrich the integration discipline in meaningful ways, that go beyond tokenism, extend love and work toward restorative justice.

Moreover, the examples provided here are only a few examples of cultures rich in the permeation of spirituality. There are so many more examples, and culture is so much more than race or ethnicity. In keeping with APA's (2017) updated Multicultural Guidelines, culture is best understood as an intersection of identities and experiences. At minimum, the identities considered must include those in Pamela Hays's (2008) ADDRESSING model: Age, Developmental and acquired Disabilities, Religion, Ethnicity, Socioeconomic status, Sexual orientation, Indigenous heritage, National origin, and Gender. What we have outlined above are merely a few examples of the depth of existing spirituality and theological integration that have not been as widely incorporated into the integration literature.

As we reflect on the ways that many communities of color understand their lived experiences, whether in the United States or globally, we are reminded about how lived experience influences one's understanding of God. For example, the theme of suffering in the face of widespread systemic injustice highlighted by James Cone (2012b) being central to Black Christianity is a theme which we do not see as pervasively among integration literature in general. The theme of suffering rooted in centuries of saints' martyrdom among Latine Christians, and the invisibility among Asian Americans highlighted by Kim-Kort (2012) finding its resolution in drawing on moment-by-moment empowerment of the Holy Spirit, are rich themes that can and should enrich our understanding of psychology and the Christian faith. Yet, these voices are often not readily included in the integration conversation.

Wrapping Things Up

Back in the 1900s, approximately 82% of Christians resided in Europe and North America (Hanciles, 2008, as cited in Keener, 2011). In 2020, about two-thirds of Christians live in Asia, Africa, Latin America, and Oceania (also known as the Global South), and it is expected that by 2050, over three-quarters of Christians will live in the Global South (Zurlo et al., 2021). As a result of the global redistribution of Christianity, the Christian faith is expected to burgeon outside of the Western world, which will continue to reshape global Christianity and the practice of integration between psychology and theology. Consequently, the ways that we practice integration will need to be mindful of this growing presence of Christians globally, and the continued growing diversity of the United States. Moreover, we can work toward greater love and justice by listening to voices that have often been marginalized and addressing injustices that may have occurred within the integrative dialogue between psychology and Christian faith.

As you recall in our Cycle of Transformation, it is often an experience, our studies, or new reflections that present a new or jarring experience that we seek to grapple with. As we have seen in this chapter, some of these new experiences for you might be having a greater awareness of the injustices that have occurred in the past.

We've seen how some communities and groups of people have not had their stories represented, or have had limited resources to draw on, to make sense of their own story and history compared with majority communities.

Contextual theologies remind us of a foundational point: as Christians working within psychology, we show love and work toward justice by affirming the full humanity of each person. Recalling our understanding of Christian justice, if there are those that are suffering or are oppressed, we have a duty to show love by first listening and seeking to understand, then taking action toward justice. As we begin to listen to others and to silenced parts of ourselves, we are changed in the process and become a conduit of healing and justice in our churches, community, and wider society. Christian theological reflections from the different contexts that we have briefly surveyed here are by no means an attempt to summarize the richness and depth of each one of these contexts. Rather they provide us a starting point for further exploration into how these and many other voices have something essential to contribute to both Christian theology and psychological reflection.

Practicing integration that is oriented toward love of neighbor means that we work toward restorative justice by eliminating systemic factors that create conditions for injustice (Callaway & Whitney, 2022). Moreover, as we engage in an intentional process of reflecting on our stories about areas that might have been silenced in the past, we allow God's redemptive and restorative justice to take place. Further, as we actively engage contextual theologies, we broaden the narratives of how Christian integration is practiced by including a wider range of human experiences that enrich the integration dialogue. We hope that future generations of scholars and psychologists will be better able to understand how their own integration journey interacts with their cultural background and milieu. We also hope that in doing so, we will create a more hermeneutically just literature to inform integration both at the personal and communal levels.

Reflection Questions

1. What is hermeneutical injustice? Are there ways that you can personally relate to the idea of hermeneutical injustice? Why is hermeneutical injustice important for our conversation about integration?

2. In this chapter you read about theological perspectives from various BIPOC. Which ones were most familiar to you? Which ones were least familiar to you? When you reflect on these various theological perspectives discussed in this chapter, what do you find most exciting? What do you find most challenging? Why?

3. What are some ways that these various theological perspectives can inform and/or broaden your faith perspective? Your research or practice within psychology?

Holding Space for Lament in the Face of Injustice

Lament recognizes the struggles of life and
cries out for justice against existing injustices.

SOONG-CHAN RAH (2015)

On March 16, 2021, Robert Aaron Long went into three different massage parlors in the Atlanta metro area and fired gunshots, killing Daoyou Feng, Hyun Jung Grant, Suncha Kim, Paul Andre Michels, Soon Chung Park, Xiaojie Tan, Delaina Ashley Yaun, and Yong Ae Yue (BBC, 2021, March). Long also shot and severely injured Elcias Hernandez-Ortiz (BBC, 2021, March). Six of the victims were women of Asian descent, who were at work when Long intruded and engaged in a shooting spree. This horrific murder followed a long season of anti-Asian sentiments which began to intensify in March 2020 and involved assaults against Asians and Asian Americans in the United States, many of whom were elderly (BBC, 2021, May; Leung, 2021). In fact, the Center for Study of Hate and Extremism at California State University (San Bernardino) reported that when comparing the first quarter of 2020 (January-April) with the first quarter of the year in 2021, there was a 164% increase in reports of hate crimes against Asian Americans (Smith, 2021, May 21). Some of these physical assaults also resulted in death (Leung, 2021, CBS SF, 2021). In the wake of this murder, I (Carissa) wrestled with shock, sorrow, and disorientation as I reflected on my existence as an Asian woman. Within a few days of the shooting in Atlanta, I received a text from a friend saying, "I am mad, I am sad, and I am scared to go out. I don't want my daughter to live in this kind of world." As a mother of an Asian American daughter, I can understand this at a deep level. We were both grappling with this reality and our fears. That week, while I was feeding, playing, and interacting with my daughter, I found myself thinking about the women who were killed by Long, how at one point, they too were babies—fed and cared for by their parents. I also found myself wondering what kind of world my daughter would be growing up in. Is it safe?

The sad reality is that these race-based assaults and the Atlanta shootings are not the only ones of their kind. Other racially motivated shootings have taken place in the United States. On June 17, 2015, nine Black men and women were shot and killed during a Bible study at the Emanuel African Methodist Episcopal Church (Corasaniti et al., 2015). On August 3, 2019, a mass shooting targeting Mexican Americans occurred in El Paso, killing twenty-three people and injuring twenty-two others (Attanasio, 2020; Crabtree, 2021). In the last decade alone, we have mourned the untimely and senseless deaths of many Black Americans: Tamir Rice, Atatiana Jefferson, Walter Scott, Eric Garner, Yvette Smith, Laquan MacDonald, Mike Brown, Sandra Bland, Alton Sterling, Freddie Gray, George Floyd, Breonna Taylor, Ahmaud Arbery, and Tyre Nichols (Neason, 2020). This is just to name some out of the many, many others.

As mentioned throughout the book, our understanding of the integration of psychology and theology means that we are moved as people and as a community of Christians to address the realities of injustice in our society, by extending love and working toward justice. However, this can be so hard when we find ourselves shocked, scared, or even traumatized by injustices that occur. One of the most difficult aspects of our lives is being confronted with pain, suffering, and injustice. At the same time, God does not deny our pain and suffering, and Scripture is not silent about the pain or injustice that occurs in the world. The Bible is full of stories of people who are oppressed, exiled, displaced, or migrant, and those who are subjected to systemic injustices, discrimination, and senseless death. We know that Scripture does have something to say about senseless killings and injustices in our society—and certainly psychology (which is a science that makes sense of human behavior, including prejudices, pain, grief, and agony) has something to say about this egregious pain in our racialized world. Consequently, if we are careful to remember this, our work within integration has much to contribute to the conversation about injustice, pain, and suffering in our society.

In this chapter we will describe: (1) how the concept of liminal space helps us make sense of sufferings and injustices in this world, (2) how we are to respond to these injustices from a biblical perspective, and (3) how lament ultimately shapes us toward the goal of becoming integrated persons.[1]

---

[1]We are indebted to Drs. Elizabeth Hall, Megan Anna Neff, and Mark McMinn for their work on lament, which accurately situates lament as a uniquely Christian and integrative response to suffering and evil that holds potential for spiritual transformation. See further L. Hall, 2016, and Neff & McMinn, 2020.

Key Concept 7.1

Moving toward an integrated view
of pain and suffering means we must
learn to live in the liminal space of
lament and restorative hope.

Any discussion of pain, suffering, and injustice from the stand-point of integration will naturally involve Christ's death, the cross, and resurrection. Both Good Friday and Easter are important for our discussion here.

How does your family prepare for Good Friday and Easter? In my (Carissa's) family, Easter was on our minds for weeks or months before the day itself. My family, church, and community prepared ourselves in significant ways for Easter Sunday (e.g., decorating eggs, buying new clothes, preparing for the Easter Sunday choir performance, and egg hunts). It was curious to me that Good Friday, in many ways, received very little attention and preparation, com-pared to Easter Sunday. For Good Friday, we would go to church, reflect on biblical passages and hymns with themes of Christ's death on the cross. We would leave service that day, knowing that we would come back on Sunday for a festive celebration. Even more curious than the way my church prepared for Good Friday was its silence about the Saturday in between. In my family, we did not talk about the significance of that Saturday, and we just went about our day as if it was a normal Saturday, visiting grandparents or playing with friends. This in-between (or liminal) day is what we would like to draw your attention to. *Liminal* comes from the Latin word *līmen,* which translates to "threshold" (Dictionary.com, n.d.).

The term liminality was first coined by anthropologist Arnold Van Gennep in 1909 to describe *transitions*, or the spaces in between (Turner, 1974). In the Christian faith, one of the most poignant representations of the liminal space is Holy Saturday, which is the day between Good Friday and Easter.

Various Christian denominations, especially the Catholic and Eastern Orthodox churches, recognize Holy Saturday as an important day signifying the end of Lent. Historically, these denominations have held a special Easter Vigil where fires or candles are lit to symbolize Christ dying and moving toward his resurrected life. The Easter Vigil recognizes this time between death and new life. We won't get into the historical reasons most Christian churches have slowly let go of the tradition of Holy Saturday here, but we would like to propose that the significance of Holy Saturday needs to be brought back, especially as we reflect on racial injustices. The Reverend Doctor Pamela Cooper-White (2014), in contrasting Holy Saturday to both Good Friday and Easter Sunday, states the following:

> Holy Saturday is different. It's quiet, not full of drama or big, important music. It's the "between" that spans the agony of Good Friday and the overwhelming joy of Easter. While we have hindsight that Jesus' family and friends did not have—we know that this story has a miraculous ending that no one could then foresee (except Jesus himself, and on Thursday and Friday even Jesus had his doubts and fears)—we also perhaps need a little time—to process all that has happened this past Holy Week, to digest the reality of Jesus' death—yes, he really died! That wasn't just a magic show where the beautiful young woman appears to be sawed in half but then rises out of the magician's box and we

know it was all just an illusion. Jesus really died—and if we believe in Jesus as the incarnation of God, we must also proclaim that *God* died there on that hideous Roman cross, an instrument of ingenious, sadistic slow death. *God's own self*, today, is dead, lying in a borrowed tomb. (p. 2)

When I (Carissa) read the Reverend Doctor Pamela Cooper-White's homily a number of years ago, it was the first time I reflected on how Jesus' followers, mother, and siblings must have felt on the day after his death: the shock, sorrow, disorientation, and the question of "Now what?" Jesus' followers did not know that Jesus was going to be resurrected the next day, and in between Friday and Sunday, they lived in grief and horror. From time to time in our lives, grief and tragedy ruthlessly jolt us out of our expectations, assumptions, and beliefs. We often want to go straight into action (and at times, this is appropriate), but in our contemporary times, we often have lost the art of being in the in-between space, to mourn, process, and catch up with the reality that we are living in.

The jolting events or crisis could be the loss of a loved one, an accident, being diagnosed with a chronic or terminal illness, a traumatic event, discovering infidelity by a spouse, divorce in the family, the list goes on and on. Sometimes, this jolt comes from a national tragedy, whether it be 9/11, the COVID-19 pandemic, mass shootings in the country, or the apparent pattern that certain minority communities are at greater risks of assaults or deaths. Whatever the event is, this jolting event represents a death: the death of expectations, assumptions, or beliefs.

We described this kind of jolting or jarring event in chapter five in reference to the Cycle of Transformation. These jarring events cause us to reevaluate our views of God, self, and others. What we didn't mention much in chapter five is that sometimes we sit in this uncomfortable space for a while (sometimes a very long time), and we don't always move quickly toward new understanding or meaning-making. Our Christian faith provides a space for us to understand the pain and disorientation after a crisis where core beliefs are disrupted and challenged. Holy Saturday represents a time when we sit with our complex or conflicting thoughts and feelings, as well as the pain and the injustice that we feel after a crisis. When we think back to Jesus' own disciples after his death on Friday, we know that there are others who have waited in pain and suffering and longed for healing, wholeness, and restoration. This brings us to an important takeaway from our Christian faith, namely, that pain, injustice, and crisis are not things that God overlooks or glosses over. Even though God created the world as good in the beginning, pain and injustice are a reality as we live in this time in-between Jesus' first and second comings.

As I (Carissa) became more aware of the increasing violence toward the Asian American elderly communities in and around San Francisco, Los Angeles, New York, and many other Asian communities all over the United States, I was absolutely shocked. My core belief that I and others who look like me were physically and emotionally safe was disrupted. I had to accept the reality that people who look like me could be targeted for physical assault or worse. This Holy Saturday moment was disruptive and unsettling, and for me, there was much mourning, grieving, wailing to God to adjust to this new reality. In this moment, my emotions had to be expressed and processed in light of this realization, or "to digest the reality" (Cooper-White, 2014, p. 2) of the death of my core belief related to my own safety and security, and that of my family.

Holy Saturday reminds us that we live in the tension between death and life, between grief and hope. Ultimately, Holy Saturday is not where we stay because it points to Easter Sunday, where we experience Christ's victory over death, sin, and unrighteousness (on an individual and systemic level). In many ways, though, liminality still represents the reality of our lives as followers of Jesus Christ. While Easter has taken place and Christ has risen from the dead, we are still looking forward to yet another new reality, which is glorification or Christ's second coming. On that day, creation will be restored and will be as it should be. But today, we live in the day post-resurrection, but pre-glorification, which is a transitional space. Following Christ's resurrection from the dead, we live in this new reality of Christ's victory over sin while diligently working out what that looks like in our lives, community, vocation, and the world. As we await new creation, we are encouraged by the fact that in Christ there is true victory, and that our work to restore relationships and lives is not in vain.

Key Concept 7.2

Lament is an integrative response to suffering and injustice.

If you have ever sat with someone encountering physical or emotional pain? Or if you have encountered physical or emotional pain yourself, you'll know that any kind of theoretical answers for why pain or suffering is happening are largely unhelpful. You might even know firsthand how it can actually make our suffering worse to have someone try to "fix" things or provide a quick solution or explanation when we are in pain. I (William) remember attending the funeral of someone dearly loved in our community. All of us were grieving the loss of this loved one as we gathered that Friday to remember this friend who had meant so much to us, and yet, as the pastor gave the funeral message, he did not acknowledge the grief that was actually occurring for those in attendance. Even though everyone was hurting, the funeral message was: "Don't be sad. This should be a day of celebration because this person is at home with Jesus." I remember feeling the discontinuity between what the pastor was saying and what I was feeling. While it was true that our friend was at home with God, the reality for those of us still on earth was that we were deeply hurting.

As we've mentioned, one of the unique aspects of the Christian faith is that it does not dismiss pain, suffering, or evil. As Christians, we are offered a unique perspective. God is not a God who stands apart from us while we suffer. In fact, God is one who takes on human flesh and suffers along with us. According to Jürgen Moltmann in *The Crucified God* (1993), God is a God who suffers alongside those who are disinherited, hurt, and suffering. God's solidarity with those who are in pain is evidenced by Christ's death on the cross. God does not discount pain and suffering, but enters into human pain, and relates to our own sufferings (Psalm 22:24; Hebrews 4:15-16). One day, God will ultimately destroy all pain and suffering (Revelation 21:3-4). For Christians, there is hope. Christian hope looks forward to the day when evil will be destroyed forever, and yet, we do not deny that pain and injustice is part of the human experience (Neff & McMinn, 2020). Fortunately, we have in Scripture examples of what it means to sit with those who are in pain. Scripture provides us with an alternative theological vision for suffering and evil that can be extremely helpful when we encounter pain, suffering, and injustice: lament.

Several features of lament are vital to note as we begin to explore this topic as a response to pain and injustice.

First, it is important to remember that lament is not merely grieving or mourning. While lament does include grieving and mourning, a unique feature of lament is that it is directed toward God, as a mode of direct communication with him (Swinton, 2007; Hall, 2016). Katongole and Rice (2008) aptly note, "Lament . . . is not a cry into a void. Lament is a cry directed to God. It is the cry of those who see the truth of the world's deep wounds and the cost of seeking peace. It is the prayer of those who are deeply disturbed by the way things are" (p. 78).

If you read some of the psalms of lament, you will notice first and foremost that these cries and complaints are directed to God. Psalms 90:13; 94:3; 119:84 give you a brief sample of the types of psalms of lament that we are talking about here. The psalms of lament contain phrases like: "Make this stop, God! Why did this happen, God? Where were you, God? How long does this have to continue, God?" When you read these psalms, the anguish and intensity is real and palpable, and it is clear that this pain is directed to the One that the psalmist believes has control over earthly events. Psalm 142 provides such a description of the psalmist's pain being communicated toward God:

I cry aloud to the Lord;
　I lift up my voice to the Lord for mercy.
I pour out before him my complaint;
　before him I tell my trouble.

When my spirit grows faint within me,

> it is you who watch over my way. (Psalm 142:1-3)

As students of psychology, you will encounter human pain, suffering, and injustices in your career. For the Christian, one of the responses to pain is to direct it toward God. This can be our pain, the pain of others, or the injustices in the world. It is okay to communicate with God *in* our suffering and pain and *about* our suffering and pain. When teaching, we often find that students feel they have to be polite or use the right words to pray and talk with God about pain, or that they have to come to some sort of resolution and be composed enough in some way. When we engage in lament, we acknowledge that the world is not as it was intended to be and that God knows and hears the depths of our feelings and thoughts, even those we would rather deny.

While some elements of church culture might lead us to think that we have to deny or not talk about the pain that we experience, the psalms present a stark contrast to this (Hall, 2016). Notice above that the psalmist "cries" out and "pours" out complaint in Psalm 142. These are not descriptions of someone who is overly composed or has a resolution to the suffering and injustice that they are feeling. Lament remains an important way for us to communicate with God about pain, suffering, and injustice that we or someone else is experiencing (Hall, 2016; Neff & McMinn, 2020).

Second, it is important to note that lament is a way to articulate pain and suffering (Brueggemann, 1995; Hall, 2016). God not only allows us to lament, but he also encourages us and guides us to put words to the evil and injustice in the world. Old Testament scholar Walter Brueggemann aptly notes that about a third of the book of Psalms actually consists of lament psalms (Brueggemann, 1986).

When we remember that the Psalms were used in Israel's corporate worship, it is clear from the sheer amount of these lament psalms that God does not want us to be silent in the face of pain and suffering. In his paper "The Costly Loss of Lament," Walter Brueggemann (1986) argues that we can understand praise only if we truly understand and allow ourselves to enter into lament and give voice to our pain and suffering. Not engaging in lament is a failure to bring our true selves before God, and to be silent in times that we should not be. Lament becomes an important way to give voice to pain, suffering, anger, and injustice—even when the words might be hard to find.

In the psychological literature, many have discussed the importance of becoming aware of emotions and putting words to them. One of the reasons that has been most widely cited is that denying our emotions takes up energy that can otherwise be invested in joy, creativity, and aspirations (McWilliams, 2011). Further, recent research has shown that cutting off emotions from awareness is linked to a greater possibility of aggression among offenders (Roberton et al., 2015), indicating that our efforts in suppressing emotions are often unsuccessful (McWilliams, 2011). In addition, an experiment on patients who suffer from chronic pain revealed that suppressing anger was linked to a greater experience of pain (Burns et al., 2008). These are just a few examples of the ways in which suppressing emotions actually leads to undesirable outcomes. We are created as humans with bodies that alert us to dangers, threats, and pain, and to allow ourselves to experience these responses is to recruit the fullness of human faculty that God has gifted us. The research cited above shows that having an integrated response—including our thoughts, feelings, and sensations—is an adaptive process that allows us to heal in a more natural way (van der Kolk, 2014).

Most importantly, expressing our true emotions within safe and secure relationships is not only healthy, but brings us into deeper authenticity in these interpersonal contexts. Donald Winnicott (1965), a prominent psychoanalytic thinker who focused much of his work on child-mother relationships, made the distinction between false self and true self. He argues that when a child is able to express uncomfortable feelings toward the mother, the child is enabled to experience an authentic version of themselves. In essence, through the process of expressing these feelings (distress, fear, anger, etc.), the child comes to know themselves and their mother better, and as such, they enter into a deeper intimacy in this parent-child dyad. It is the same way in our relationship with God. If we are only able to bring praise before God but not our lament, we are cultivating an inauthentic relationship with him (Brueggemann, 1995).

 Key Concept 7.3

Lament is a way to articulate the pain and suffering we feel about the evil and injustices we experience in the world.

Third, within Scripture, lament is both a personal and communal process. We can practice lamenting both individually and collectively. We can lament our own pain, our own unrighteousness, the pain of others, and the pain and injustice inflicted by systems or societies. As mentioned above, the lament psalms make up a large portion of the book of Psalms and were used in corporate worship, and we even have a whole book of the Bible dedicated to lament (the book of Lamentations). Even though lament is clearly recognized in Scripture, the American church has the tendency to avoid lament in their collective worship, and many Christians in America neglect lament in their personal lives. In Soong-Chan Rah's incisive work *Prophetic Lament: A Challenge to the Western Church* (2015), he observes that the loss of lament in the American church "reflects a serious theological deficiency" (p. 22). Losing lament in our church life can result in an incorrect message that anger, pain, and sadness do not have a place in worship or our personal spiritual lives.

We mentioned earlier how we as authors understand integration as an embodied practice where we bring our full humanity and human experience to the table. When we avoid lament, and neglect appropriately calling evil and injustice what it is, we lose the prophetic role that the church of Jesus has in guiding and leading people of faith to bring their entire lives fully before God. Soong-Chan Rah (2015) notes that minimization of lament has resulted in the loss of an important theological narrative of suffering that is part of the human experience. Rah (2015) further concludes that the "absence of lament in the liturgy of the American church results in the loss of memory. We forget the necessity of lamenting over suffering and pain. We forget the reality of suffering and pain" (p. 24).

Earlier in the chapter, we discussed how a crisis occurs when there is a disruption or a death of our core beliefs (e.g., that the world is a just place). We look toward the day of resurrection and restoration, and depending on what the jolting event or death was, this restoration looks different in each case. However, we can't plan for appropriate actions without facing reality, both cognitively and emotionally. And these cognitive and emotional responses take place in the form of lamenting the condition of this world. However, our integrative response would not be complete without also lamenting the conditions of our heart.

As difficult as it may be to lament, in doing so, we are affirming that this world is not as it was created. In chapter three, we talked about creation, fall, redemption, and then new creation. In lamenting, we are actually expressing our deep faith in a world that was designed to be good (creation) and that one day will be restored to its glorified state (new creation). Lamenting also acknowledges the truth that this world is in a liminal state: it is undergoing restoration, but it is not quite there yet. In this space of already/not yet, we grieve the individual and structural sinfulness that results in pain and injustice. When we experience the impact of the world that is broken and sinful, the only proper response is to lament, and this involves mourning and grieving. Not to do so is to be in denial, or results in a loss of memory, as Soon-Chan Rah noted.

So, for me (Carissa), when the shootings happened in Atlanta, I grieved and lamented. I allowed myself to feel the sadness for the lives lost and their families. I grieved for my Asian/Asian American friends and family who have to then experience the fear of possibly being assaulted when they are going about their day. The biblical lament involves grieving and mourning, but as we mentioned, it also stretches beyond this. By engaging in lament, we bring our pain and protest before and communicate with God, giving voice to our pain and suffering in a new way. This moves lament from a personal/individual process to a relational process before God and others in our collective Christian community.

Further, through engaging in lament, we are entering into a process by which we are able to participate in authentic praise (Brueggemann, 1995; Hall, 2016). Eugene Peterson (1991, p. 122, as cited in Hall, 2016) states, "All true prayer pursued far enough will become praise. . . . It does not always get there quickly. It does not always get there easily. . . . But the end is always praise." When we look at psalms of lament in the Bible, we also see a structure in which the sufferer begins with a complaint and ends it with praise and confidence in the character of God, regardless of whether the suffering has been resolved (Hall, 2016). Lament is a process by which we enter into the depth of our suffering with God, knowing that God understands pain and grief.

How Does Lament Relate to Racial Injustice?

Lamenting in the face of racism is important because in doing so, we acknowledge that this world is not as it was created to be.[2] We also acknowledge that this is not how creation will always be, as shown in the vision of kingdom of God in the book of Revelation, where racial, ethnic, and national differences are not erased, but exist in harmony as people worship God. As such, we acknowledge the liminality of our present condition. Not only do we acknowledge this cognitively, but we also face this reality with our emotions (Muthiah, 2021), and therefore engage in an embodied process of facing the terrible reality of racism. We don't just stand from an

---

[2]In this chapter we have primarily focused on racial injustices. However, as we have referenced in this section, injustices occur in many other areas as well, in the forms of ableism, ageism, sexism, religious persecution, homophobia, etc. We have chosen to focus on one aspect of the ADDRESSING factor to discuss injustices as one example of lament as an integrative response to injustices. However, the main point in this chapter is that lament is an integrative response to injustices of all kinds. Many parts of the Bible, such as the book of Lamentations and the psalms of lament, provide examples of lament as a response to multiple kinds of injustices and oppressions.

analytic distance stating that racism is wrong; we are ached by this reality, and groan for God to restore this world (Billings, 2016).

Lament holds such power because when we are willing to enter into this reality emotionally as well as cognitively, we are better able to empathize with others who may have experiences different from ours. If you remember from chapter five, all of us have differing experiences of the world partially because of our ADDRESSING factors. Some identities are more privileged than others, which often blinds us to others' less-privileged experiences. Depending on the color of our skin, gender, age, and so on, we are all subjected to different realities of racism. For example, while anti-Asian racism was heightening, I (Carissa) was aware and a little more nervous about the possibility of being assaulted while I was out. This reality is different for William, who is White and male, and doesn't carry the same level of nervousness or vigilance. This can be generalized into other experiences as well. There are experiences that I (Carissa) have not had personally or worries I do not carry due to privileges. For instance, I (Carissa) have the privilege of being part of a religious majority in the United States where I can easily find a place to worship among many different Christian churches. In lamenting, we allow ourselves to be impacted emotionally by the reality of racism and other injustices, which opens up the space for us to empathize with others, who may have radically different experiences than we do (Muthiah, 2021).

Lamenting because of racism helps us become more fully integrated people. The way we as Christians deal with racism often falls into one of two pitfalls: silence and denial, or self-reliance. On one hand, silence or denial occurs when churches and

Christian institutions do not acknowledge racism and stay silent even in the wake of significant national tragedies, such as the shooting at the Charleston African Methodist Episcopal church in 2015. Perhaps we are silent because we do not know what to say, but meanwhile, there are members of our congregations or communities who feel alone in their pain and despair for not having racism named in these instances. At times, when we feel overwhelmed by the magnitude of pain and injustice, it may feel more comfortable to be in denial about it or be in denial that anything could be done to make a difference. On the other hand, we can sometimes be too self-reliant and not understand that our faith is an important part of us working toward justice. For instance, sometimes when we feel anger at racism, we may channel our anger into mobilizing resources to "do something" about the problem or expressing our opinions on social media (neither of which is inherently a bad thing). However, we may rarely bring our anger, groaning, and pain to God. We may never even find spaces in our spiritual communities to lament and work for justice. Perhaps due to many churches' failure in actively addressing racism, Christians sometimes assume that God stands apart from issues of racism and discrimination, so if we want to see progress, we need to get it done ourselves. Neither silence, nor denial, nor self-reliance is a true expression of developing our integrative identities. Lament is a point of juxtaposition where our cognition and emotion meet, our lived experience and our biblical vision intersect. It provides us with another option besides denial and self-reliance. In lamenting racism, we go to the God who cares to hear our cries, the God who is able to move on our behalf. We bring our raw emotions first and foremost to God. As we do, we find that there is an action that flows from this work of lament: a greater awareness of others around us, and a desire to work toward expressing God's love and justice in the contexts and communities where God has placed us.

When churches do not actively engage in conversations about racism and work for justice, they have actively *dis*-integrated lived experience from the so-called biblical ideals (Neff & McMinn, 2020). What is preached at the pulpit does not meet the lived experience of its congregations. In ignoring the realities of racism, churches and Christian institutions inadvertently communicate the message that pains of racism, and even the reality of racism, should not be brought before God or talked about in the church.

Some of the most painful parts of the story of racism come in rightly acknowledging the White Christian church's role in the United States in promoting and defending racist ideas and practices. For instance, I (William) grew up in a Southern Baptist church in Texas. The Southern Baptist denomination is currently still the largest evangelical Protestant denomination in the United States today (Pew Research, 2019). What is often less well-known is that the Southern Baptist denomination was formed in 1845 after a split from Northern Baptists over the issue of slavery (Noll, 2019; Pew Research, 2019). Northern Baptists could not agree that missionaries could be slaveholders, while Southern Baptists vigorously argued that missionaries could own slaves. In fact, Southern Baptists defended their separation from Northern Baptists because they believed that slaveholding was both moral and legitimate (McBeth, 1987; Noll, 2019). The Bible was used to support their views of slavery (Noll, 1998). A recent report (2018) from Southern Seminary details how all of Southern Seminary's founding faculty owned slaves (see further Southern Seminary Special Report: Racism and the History of Slavery, 2018).

Growing up Southern Baptist, I didn't hear about this history though. If there was mention of slavery as part of the history of the denomination, it was quickly brushed aside, and I remember even learning that it was not a central issue. It was not until I took classes in church history in seminary that I learned how slavery was not a side issue but *the* issue that prompted the formation of the denomination (McBeth, 1987). It was not until 1995 that the Southern Baptist Convention issued a formal apology for their proslavery past (130 years later). The Southern Baptist church is just one example though. As Robert Jones (2020) correctly notes, virtually all major White Protestant denominations split over the issue of slavery.

This painful history that I (William) just described is also an example of hermeneutical injustice. Remember that hermeneutical injustices occur when there are gaps in interpretive resources which disadvantage others (Fricker, 2007). Thus, when the history is not told about White Christianity's participation in racist ideas and slavery within our collective US church history, it blinds Christians to reality and obscures the history of marginalization, oppression, and traumatization of African Americans from our collective memory as followers of Christ. In short, one of the reasons many White churches have remained silent about issues of racism for too long is that there has been a collective history of diminishing and denying the history of racism and slavery within the church. The field of integration has not always emphasized cultural awareness or worked toward justice, but one of the primary reasons for this is that the Christian theology it integrated is based on an inherited church history that has (intentionally or unintentionally) diminished and downplayed the White church's role in staying silent toward (or even promoting) issues like slavery. Just like my (William's) story about how my own church never mentioned it, many White churches and traditions have inherited a church history that conveniently leaves out these facts regarding racism.

Key Concept 7.4

As we practice lament, we hold space for our suffering and other people's suffering.

So, we have talked about how integration involves coming to terms with our cultural backgrounds—this still holds true. However, if we are honest, there are elements of our cultural and theological backgrounds related to a history of racism within the White church that we need to name as evil and sinful. We have to admit that many of our White church leaders in US Protestant history practiced an incredibly *dis*-integrated theology as they preached about the importance of salvation through Christ and love of neighbor on Sunday and actively engaged in the oppression and brutalization of African Americans throughout the week (Cone, 2012a).

Putting it into practice: Lamenting individual prejudices within our own hearts. In his book *The Deeply Formed Life*, Rich Villodas (2020) highlights the reality that all of us, regardless of our ADDRESSING factors, have individual racial prejudices. We all have biases that have been shaped by our history, context, family stories, experiences, and so on. (Villodas, 2020). Villodas contrasts this with institutional racism, which is individual prejudices that are paired with power (Emerson, 2010, as cited in Villodas, 2020). In chapter four, we described the ways that some ADDRESSING factors are more privileged than others, and when this interacts with power, those who are not in dominant positions are often left with fewer resources (whether it be hermeneutical, economic, or political). However, whether we have power or not, we all carry individual prejudices. As we close this chapter, we would like to encourage you to turn your attention on individual prejudices that exist within your own heart and to practice lamenting this reality. In this book, we have unpacked our deep beliefs that integration can't fully take place unless we are mindful of our embodied existence in this world. This encompasses our experiences and culture (inclusive of our ADDRESSING identity), in addition to our academic learning of theology and psychology. The realities of racial injustices are not excluded.

We live in a society that is pragmatically oriented. When there is a problem, we want to know what to *do*. It is important that our first step toward fixing the problem of racial injustice should incorporate what Scripture and psychology provide as a guide about how to respond to complex situations. Based on what we have unpacked in this chapter, we believe that practicing lament can help us develop our integrative identity and bring our full authentic self to God and our community. Note that being authentic here includes a growing capacity to confess our sins before God and others, and practice humility and compassion. As we all continue to practice confession and lament, we cultivate an expanded ability to be present with others and to acknowledge our biases and privileges. Ultimately, lamenting our prejudices and the racism in our society opens the pathway for us to be more present with our emotional experiences, which in turn, opens the way for us to be more present in others' suffering.

Wrapping Things Up

In this chapter, we have attempted to outline the ways liminality helps us make sense of pain, suffering, and racial injustices, and how lament is an integrative response to the agony of being in a kingdom reality that is already/not yet. Lamenting is a unique integrative Christian response that holds the potential to transform us, and as we are transformed, God uses us to effect changes in our surroundings for greater love, shalom, and justice. Ultimately, Holy Saturday is not where the story ends. Holy Saturday points us toward Easter, Christ's victory over death, pain, suffering, and injustices. By creating space for lament and liminality, we are affirming that the realities of this world are just one part of the greater story of the kingdom of God. Christ is even now transforming the world to bring it toward a full restoration in his second coming, and he invites us to partner with him in our vocation, which is a topic we will focus on in our final chapter. We hope that, by engaging in a rhythm of lament, you are expanding your capacity to enter into deeper authenticity with God, yourself, and others, and that your advocacy for racial justice would come from a deeply rooted and integrated inner life.

Reflection Questions

1. Was the concept of lament new to you? If so, what did you find that was significant about the practice? What was challenging about the practice? If the concept was not new, has your thinking about it changed any after reading the chapter? How?

2. We discussed how lament is a way to articulate the pain and suffering that we feel about the evil and injustices we experience in the world. What do you think about this? How might this practice change the way that you relate to God, others, and yourself?

3. Are there parts of your told or untold stories that need to be lamented? Either by yourself (journaling) or with a friend, describe some of these stories or parts of your life that need to be lamented. After you are finished, describe what this experience was like.

4. Lament acknowledges that the world is undergoing restoration, but it is not quite there yet. In this space of already/not yet, we can grieve the individual and structural evil and sinfulness that results in pain and injustice. What other individual and/or structural elements of evil and sinfulness come to mind that need to be grieved for you as an individual or as a community? You might want to spend a few moments writing down your own lament to God. After finishing, take a few moments: What might God be saying to you as you have engaged with this process of grief and lament?

Reflection, Action, Vocation

Finding Your Integrative Voice

The first thing is to be honest with yourself. You can never have an impact on society if you have not changed yourself. Great peacemakers are all people of integrity, of honesty, and humility.

NELSON MANDELA

The Church is the Church only when it exists for others . . . not dominating, but helping and serving. It must tell men [and women] of every calling what it means to live for Christ, to exist for others.

DIETRICH BONHOEFFER

Several years after completing graduate school and getting licensed as a clinical psychologist, I (Carissa) felt I was ready to take on another challenge, and decided I would take up a new language. I chose Mandarin. The Rosetta Stone package I purchased came with a headset where I could listen to a native speaker pronounce various words, so I in turn, could practice my pronunciation. For each word, the program would give me feedback, with a green button that appeared every time I correctly pronounced a word. I diligently practiced my vocabulary and pronunciation, and I must say, I was doing great! At the end of each module, I would get a total score, and I either got 100% or pretty close to it. The next step was to meet virtually with a native speaker instructor and a small group of other students where we would only speak in Mandarin, with no English allowed. I had practiced basic conversational phrases and words, and felt excited to finally use them with a live group. On the day of my live session, I logged in early with my headset in place. The instructor logged in with a warm smile and greeted us. She called my name and asked me a question that I understood and had practiced the answer to. I excitedly spoke my practiced phrase. She looked at me with a blank stare. She repeated her question, and I began to panic internally. I took a deep breath and repeated my answer again. She gave me a blank stare again. I could not believe what was happening; how embarrassing!

Finally, she gathered from my broken pronunciation what I was trying to say. She said her phrase again and showed me how to correctly pronounce it. I repeated it after her, but I was met with another blank stare. It was clear from that session that I did not know how to pronounce these words in Mandarin despite the affirming green buttons I had repeatedly seen during my practice!

We find that something similar happens with interdisciplinary work between psychology and the Christian faith. While there are many different ways that we can approach psychology and our Christian faith, we don't really know how to do it until we practice it in the real world with others. While we can learn a lot when we reflect on our faith, psychology, and culture, we learn a lot more as we practice integration in a community with others—just like getting personal feedback from a Mandarin speaker instead of a machine!

As authors, we find ourselves inspired by the heart that students bring into choosing this discipline of psychology. Many of our students view their work and career as sacred, and they choose psychology because this is an avenue by which they feel they are able to serve God and others well. Both of us believe that actively engaging in integration allows us to develop as individuals and helps us discover and lean into our vocation. Letting our faith inform our psychology can enrich the way we engage with our study and work, which ultimately allows us to serve our clients, community, and others well.

The purpose of this chapter is to help you understand your vocation more deeply, and to feel more comfortable with finding your own voice within the integration dialogue. First, this chapter will help orient our integrative vision as one of moving from theory toward action. Second, we will discuss how integration itself is a contextual enterprise. That is, those who are engaging in the integration dialogue are always doing it from a particular context, and this context also makes a difference to what the interdisciplinary work between the Christian faith and psychology looks like in the real world. Finally, this chapter will explore what it means for you to work toward greater love and justice within the particular context where you are situated—which is the idea of vocation or calling. Deeply reflecting on psychology, culture, and our Christian faith should move us toward acting in a more loving and just manner where we live and work.

From Theory to Action

Our early experiences of teaching integration of psychology and the Christian faith were marked by one common theme of feedback among our students that went something like this: We would begin the semester defining integration. Students would read the Five Views book where five different models of integration are discussed (Johnson, 2010).[1] As a class we would read and talk about the various models that were out there, and this would usually be followed by discussions about what model or view of integration that students leaned toward. Students would ask questions about the various approaches with interest. Ultimately though, discussions would often end with a very practical question asked by students: "Now that I understand integration from this viewpoint, how do I actually practice integration for myself?"

 Key Concept 8.1

> Developing our integrative identity
> should move us from merely thinking
> or talking about the subject to
> practicing and living out our faith
> and psychology in the particular
> context where we find ourselves.

Given the diversity found among our students, this practical question that our students ask lies at the heart of what this book is about and what we believe is vital for helping the next generation of integrative thinkers. That is, integration is an embodied practice

---

[1]The helpful and popular work *Psychology and Christianity: Five views* (2010), edited by Eric Johnson, proposes five different viewpoints on how Christian faith integration should be done. Each viewpoint provides helpful features that demonstrate the variety of ways it can take place.

of reflection and meaning-making that incorporates our Christian faith, psychology, and culture. Ultimately, developing our integrative identity within a community should move us from merely thinking or talking about the subject to having our integrative reflections prompt us toward practicing our faith and psychology in the particular context that we find ourselves in. Moreover, our hope is that as we practice our faith and psychology in this context, we will continue to be changed in the process, developing a greater capacity to love God and others and finding new ways of working toward greater justice in this particular context.

As we have guided you throughout this book, we hope you have seen that practicing integration for oneself means starting where you are and beginning to take stock of your own faith background and traditions, your studies in psychology, and your cultural context. This process helps shape our integrative identity. None of us come to the table with all our integrative views fully formed. Often, we are plunged into this process when a new or jarring experience forces us to make meaning of a situation in a new way (as described in our Cycle of Transformation). However, as we have noted in the last half of the book, making meaning of new situations often causes us to reevaluate, assimilate, or accommodate what we have known before. Sometimes the process of meaning-making and formation that develops our integrative identity involves grief and lament, sometimes it involves discomfort and pain, sometimes it involves joy; in all cases, it involves honesty. This whole process of transformation and development of our integrative identity should lead us to action. That is, because of God's great love for us and his movement of restoration of the entire world thought Jesus Christ, our integration has a *telos* informed by our Christian faith—to have our research and clinical practice work toward love and justice in the particular context where we find ourselves (Callaway & Whitney, 2022; Dwiwardani & Whitney, 2022). Since interdisciplinary work between psychology and our Christian faith should never be abstract or disembodied, it also involves elements of spiritual formation and transformation which lead us to new ways of thinking, believing, and behaving. As we move toward the close of this book, we would like to share our hope for the next generation of integrators, especially as you think of your vocation. In order to do this well, we need to pause here and briefly look back on the history of the integration movement, to provide more clarity on what we hope the future of integration might include.

A Brief History of the Integration of Christianity and Psychology

In the book so far, we have highlighted how both theology and psychology are always done within a specific context of culture and history. We have also encouraged you to reflect on your own cultural contexts as you engage in the process of integration. At this point, it is helpful to take a step back and also remember that the integration of psychology and our Christian faith always occurs within a specific context of culture and history. In fact, the beginning of integration of Christian faith and psychology occurred within a specific time and location.

Various authors have highlighted different pioneers who each contributed to the beginnings of a formal academic discipline of psychology-Christian integration, but all seem to point to the 1950s as the inception era. For example, Hathaway and Yarhouse credit pioneers such as Hildreth Marie Cross in 1952 and Clyde and Ruth Narramore in 1954 for their book and radio program, respectively, which began the integration movement in psychology (Hathaway & Yarhouse, 2021). Brad Strawn (n.d.) credits author Fritz Kunkel as the first to use the term *integration* in 1953 to refer to the psychology-integration project. Kunkel also founded a Christian counseling center in Los Angeles.

The founding of Christian Association for Psychological Science (CAPS) in 1956, as well as integrative psychology graduate programs at such institutions as Fuller Theological Seminary and Rosemead School of Psychology in the 1960s, further propelled the growth of Christian integration in psychology (Hathaway & Yarhouse, 2021). In addition, as Hathaway and Yarhouse highlight (2021), Christian integration is not unique to psychology. These authors trace the origin of the idea of integrating faith and learning to Gabelein in 1954, though the term itself did not appear in the literature until 1975 in an article by Art Holmes (Hathaway & Yarhouse, 2021).

Many other scholars and authors came after these pioneers to further develop Christian integration as a bona fide academic discipline, in addition to journals and professional conferences dedicated to this project. It is important to note that these important pioneers were located within a specific historical period (1950s) in the United States. Specifically, many of the pioneering movements were situated in Southern California. As you review the integration literature (especially early contributions), many authors focus their work on defending the integration project and argue that psychology and Christian theology can be integrated, making a case for how to think about Christianity and psychology working together. Over the history of the movement and even now, some scholars assume the two disciplines are independent (the "independence" position), while some even argue that religion and science are in conflict with each other (the "conflict" position). For example, writers in the field of integration highlight the fact that there are camps within psychology and Christianity that would reject the integration project altogether, perceiving the two to be incompatible with one another (Hathaway & Yarhouse, 2021). Notice that the beginning of the integration movement was contextualized against the backdrop of the independence and conflict positions, and early integrators were responding to this context defending the value of interdisciplinary work between psychology and Christian theology. This is, again, a very important foundational work that integration pioneers did, that many are indebted to, including us as authors. The hard work of early integration pioneers has opened the way for integration to become a respected academic discipline that is now allowing integration scholars to build on this important foundation.

Where we think the integration project may take us next is to look beyond this backdrop of independence and conflict positions, to consider current challenges, and to observe other contexts outside the Western world where other positions may be held. To illustrate this, we will turn to an international study on the relationship between science and religion.

Looking Beyond the Independence and Conflict Positions

A fascinating and extensive study by Elaine Ecklund and colleagues (2019) challenges both the independence and conflict positions, while also demonstrating the contextualized nature of the belief that religion and science are either independent of each other, or in conflict with each other. Their study surveyed a large sample of scientists from France, Hong Kong, India, Italy, Taiwan, Turkey, the United Kingdom, and the United States. They found that about half of the scientists in each country endorsed the independence position, holding that religion and science study different aspects of reality (Ecklund et al., 2019). However, while the highest proportion of scientists (about a third) in the Western countries (France, UK, and US) endorsed the conflict position, only 9-16% in Taiwan and Hong Kong endorsed the view that religion and science were in conflict with each other. Another important finding in their study was that the majority of US scientists indicated they were religiously unaffiliated (at a much higher rate than the general population), while this discrepancy was not found in India, Hong Kong, and Taiwan (Ecklund et al., 2019). In India, there was a similar level of religiosity among scientists and the general population, while in Hong Kong and Taiwan, the proportion of religious affiliation among scientists was comparable to or exceeded that of the general public (Ecklund et al., 2019).

While Ecklund et al. (2019) are broadly speaking of religion and science, their findings point to an important reality: Much of how one sees the relationship between religion and science (or psychology and Christianity) has to do with one's culture and context. As we look beyond North America and the broader Western context, it is valuable to acknowledge that many other contexts have engaged scientific inquiry from a standpoint of finding compatibility between science and religion. It is not surprising to find that a higher proportion of US scientists, who have inherited ideals from the Enlightenment and modernity with its emphasis on rationalism and dualistic views of mind and body, believe that religion stands in conflict with the enterprise of science compared to scientists in Taiwan or Hong Kong. While much integration literature in the past has often defended against the conflict thesis, we can see how certain elements of the conflict thesis were inherited from Enlightenment ideals of a deistic or naturalistic worldview that separated the spiritual realm from the natural realm. The point is that the integration movement (specific to Christianity) comes from a certain historical context, and we stand within a certain context of practicing integration today too. This history and context (even within the field of integration) often remains unnoticed, since it is the water that we swim in. It is important to notice our context, take note of the challenges of our current time, respond to them with the guidance of the Holy Spirit, and be aware that there are other contexts in which current and future integrators are called to respond to their own contextual call. Relatedly, the point we hope to make here is that you (as a student or professional) are essential for the integration dialogue to continue in the future, and that your context and cultural identity matter to the future of the integration tradition.

Key Concept 8.2

Current research and classes on integration must demonstrate how reflections on our faith, psychology, and cultural identity can be part of the solution to real-world problems—especially for those who are marginalized, poor, or oppressed.

There are many wonderful, diverse voices that can enrich our integration efforts—if we allow these diverse voices to draw on their own methodological, theological, and cultural wisdom, and if we work to cultivate spaces (in research, teaching, and clinical practice) where these voices can be elevated and nourished. Alexis Abernethy, scholar and professor of psychology at Fuller Theological Seminary, puts it this way:

> Early efforts in integration provided a strong foundation, but may have been less open to diverse voices. Present efforts are more welcoming of diverse perspectives, but may still be less open to perspectives that may enrich integrative efforts. The metaphor of musical ensembles that includes varied musical groups is a call and challenge for future integration efforts to embrace more diversity, but also engage the creative tensions that this inclusiveness evokes. . . . Given the history of integration and its emergence from selected Christian traditions, continued openness to diverse traditions is important. . . . It may be helpful to adopt metaphors for integration that provide increased capacity for diverse perspectives and voices as this increasingly reflects current integration and hopefully its future. (Abernethy, 2012, p. 1)

One of the ways that we enrich integrative efforts is to engage our unique diverse backgrounds in theology, psychology, and cultural contexts, owning all of these parts of ourselves, and using all of these parts of our integrative identity to inform and speak into the unique situations where we are called to live and work. As Sandage and Brown (2018) rightly note, integration efforts will take "differing forms based on unique contextual considerations and a plurality of differing combinations of psychological and theological traditions" (p. 161). For Sandage and Brown, one's cultural background would also be part of these "contextual considerations" that they speak of.

We've argued throughout this book for the importance of expanding the table of integration to make it more diverse. The way we move forward with increasing diversity within integration is by allowing Christians who study psychology to actually begin the meaning-making reflection and transformation process for themselves from their own particular theological, psychological, and cultural tradition. As we allow space for this kind of reflection and meaning-making to take place (as we have introduced throughout this book), we also allow ourselves to be changed in the process by God's Spirit.

When I was a theology student, I (William) ran across a theological vision by the renowned Yale Divinity theologian Kathryn Tanner where she argued that current theological reflection needs to be focused on real-world solutions that promote human flourishing. She stated: "Theologians are now primarily called to provide, not a theoretical argument for Christianity's plausibility, but an account of how Christianity can be part of the solution, rather than simply part of the problem, on matters of great human moment that make a life-and-death difference to people, especially the poor and oppressed" (Tanner, 2010b, p. 43). We present this here because we believe that this correction for theologians is applicable to the integration movement. For the current state of integration and integration programs, we probably no longer need to spend the majority of our time defending the plausibility of Christianity and psychology working together (as we can be thankful to our early integration mentors and scholars who have carved out space for this). However, we believe that the current call for the next generation of integrators is to demonstrate how deep and diverse reflections on our faith, psychology, and cultural identity can be part of the solution to real-world problems—especially for those who are marginalized, poor, or oppressed—by working toward greater love and justice in our churches, communities, and society.

Action and Vocation

So now we turn to you, as future scholars and practitioners of integration, to consider how this vision may shape your vocation. Our journey through these chapters so far has been to help you consider the various components of integration (Christian theology/faith, psychology, and culture) and to consider how each of your stories has been impacted by each of these components of the Integration Triad. We have worked to help you prayerfully and mindfully make meaning of your own faith, experiences, and culture, and to let all of this be informed by the discipline of psychology. We have argued in this book that no real conflict exists between psychology and the Christian faith and that both can contribute to a more complete picture of the world and human person than either perspective can give on its own.

As we've seen, integration is not simply thinking about the subject of psychology and your Christian beliefs in an abstract way that is separate from our own development as individuals, our communities of interpretation, or our own spiritual formation. Developing our integrative identity involves bringing our whole selves before God and being open to what God might be saying to us to help us love him, others, and ourselves more—and hopefully open to doing this in more authentic and honest ways. Baptist theologian James McClendon (1974) says it like this: "By recognizing that Christian beliefs are not so many 'propositions' to be . . .

juggled like truth-functions in a computer, but are living convictions which give shape to actual lives and actual communities, we open ourselves to the possibility that the only relevant critical examination of Christian beliefs may be one which begins by attending to lived lives" (pp. 34-35). The stories and narratives that we inhabit (and most importantly, for this book, our integrative ones) make a difference on how actual lives and communities are shaped, and they give form to the traditions that we inhabit (MacIntyre, 2007).

Key Concept 8.3

One of the most vital results from developing our integrative identity is how this personal transformation helps us discover and understand our vocation.

As students of psychology, you also exist in a scientific community that is composed of social scientists who are interested in human thought and behavior. Many psychology researchers and professors are compelled to help others through their research, clinical practice, and work. This is all good. However, as we consider our faith as Christians, we are also situated in a particular context where we will use what we learn in psychology so that we may live out our faith in Jesus Christ in a particular way.

For Christians, actively living out Christ's love and justice in the world in a certain action-oriented way is our *vocation*—since it is clear from Scripture that what God has done for us in Jesus Christ shapes the way we act and live out our lives in the world. Romans 12:1-2 is a great snapshot of this idea of vocation in that our lives are an "offering" (The Message) and "living sacrifice" (NIV) to God. From a Christian perspective, vocation does not mean deciding on a static career choice or a task that one performs to accrue wealth or a consistent salary. It is not simply deciding whether you should get a degree in marriage and family therapy or PhD in clinical psychology. As a follower of Jesus, our vocation is responding to God's love in an active way that overflows from what God has done for us (King & Whitney, 2015). If you check out Romans 8, this kind of active engagement in the world is empowered, upheld, and sustained by God's Spirit. Any place where there is the flourishing of human life, any place where shalom is occurring, or injustices are being addressed, is a place where God's Spirit is at work (Plantinga, 2002). Responding to God's love through our vocation means we extend God's love to others in whatever context we find ourselves, and as Mark Labberton has noted, this process makes us more authentically human (Labberton, 2014).

Thus, one of the most vital results in developing our integrative identity is how it helps us understand and discover our vocation. We've argued that the *telos* of integration is that we are transformed by God and our studies in a certain way so that we can move toward loving God and others well, and work toward promoting the love and justice of God's kingdom here on earth. Jesus' ministry here on earth was about human flourishing as he provided bodily restoration, proclamation of freedom for the imprisoned, and offered freedom for the oppressed (Luke 4:18; Callaway & Whitney, 2022). Working toward the justice and love found in God's kingdom here on earth means that we are working toward the prospering and flourishing of humanity in our own particular context. As we've noted, this flourishing of the created world and human life is captured by the Hebrew word *shalom*, which we introduced in chapter three. As Christians, what we do in psychology should be centered around a desire to join the work of God to bring flourishing and shalom to our particular context within psychology. In short, finding one's vocation as a follower of Christ moves us beyond the walls of the church to reflect and reimagine how Jesus' ministry of reconciliation makes a difference for the "society, culture, and neighborhoods in which we live, and move, and have our being" (Callaway & Whitney, 2022). Our vocation should involve the knowledge that God is already working in the lives of those that have been entrusted to our care, the lives of those that we have relationships with (Neff & McMinn, 2020). Thus, vocation involves both trusting that God's Spirit is working to bring restoration in the lives of others around us, and trusting that our work, motivated and empowered by God's love and Spirit, will be used by God to contribute to healing and restoration.

In the previous chapter we discussed how lament is a unique Christian response to pain and suffering in the world that helps us become more integrated. In addition to this, we also firmly believe that practicing integration is part of discerning our vocation in the world. As students of psychology, you will have the opportunity to work toward shalom and pursue peace in a particular context with your studies and career in psychology. As you continue developing your integrative reflections, God's Spirit will speak to you and guide you into a unique form of action in the world. Thus, as we are empowered by God's Spirit, we can understand our vocation to have creative capacities that can be applied to the area of work that has been entrusted to us. In fact, as recent theologians have noted, God's Spirit brings creative, life-giving energy (Moltmann, 1997;

Johnston, 2014) that enables us to shape our particular context into "things of beauty, truth and goodness" (Gunton, 2004 p. 7). Integrative reflection and discovering our integrative identity naturally involve a greater capacity to love and work for justice, which also results in a particular kind of action of shaping the world toward shalom that can be considered our vocation. But are there certain elements that should be involved in our vocation as students of psychology and as Christians?

We believe that there are. If we really take seriously the idea that doing integration well involves loving God and neighbor, then our work within the integration of psychology and the Christian faith will naturally be oriented toward love and justice. Practicing integration means understanding the injustices that have occurred both inside and outside the church to marginalized or oppressed groups. It also means being committed to the flourishing and thriving of those who are marginalized or oppressed. Dr. Martin Luther King Jr. aptly noted, "Justice at its best is love correcting everything that stands against love" (King, 1963). We are suggesting that your vocation will naturally include loving God and neighbor, but in addition to this, your outward action of love should also involve working toward justice. Boston College theology professor Lisa Cahill (2013) notes that "both the practice of love and the theology of Christian practice must be structured by justice" (p. 248).

God's love has creative capacities to create something new, and to sustain it. Just as we can think of injustices robbing humanity of its dignity, the converse is also true—we can think of God's love and justice as creating a space where humanity can flourish. In turn, as Christians working within psychology, we have the capacity as we are empowered by God's Spirit to create something new in the area where we find ourselves working and to sustain this new space by working toward justice and love. In short, Christians working within psychology are part of shaping the realm that God has given us with the view that God is using our work to bring wholeness, restoration, peace, and justice. God's great love reaches far beyond the bounds of the church to the entire creation and all of humanity—and it is this love that desires that all people, everywhere come to know greater wholeness and abundant life. God as Creator sustains the good creation and sustains us as we continue to do our work within psychology. God speaks his continual "yes" to life as he upholds the human creature and creation from destruction, and works to bring about restoration (Moltmann, 1985).

We have already indicated that this kind of justice and advocacy is important to how we understand our integrative identity. As Callaway and Whitney (2022) note, vocation informed by a Christian understanding of justice can take four basic forms: (1) advocating for justice in the area where we are situated; (2) seeking to understand in our research or clinical work the injustices that have been experienced by various groups; (3) working to eradicate injustices in our society and organizations; and (4) working to eradicate unjust patterns of thinking, believing, or behaving that occur within individuals. We hope that throughout this book your idea of God's love has been broadened to include forms of action and awareness of those that have been marginalized or oppressed.

At a basic level, after you have read through this book, we hope that you might feel motivated to share some of your own story or reflections about your integrative identity with a small group, your church, or a friend. Or maybe you feel God leading you to pursue other actions that are justice oriented to advocate for those with mental health needs or address racial injustices and disparities in your neighborhood, college, or church community. Maybe for some of you, vocation will mean pursuing a career serving those that are marginalized in your community. Or maybe this means volunteering some of your time to help your church create, develop, and advance a program that serves those with mental health needs. New Testament scholar William Barclay famously said that a saint is someone whose life makes it easier for others to believe in God (Barclay, 1976). We like this idea, since developing our integrative identity, being led by God's Spirit, and working toward restoration in the context where we have been placed means that we are making it a little easier for others to believe in God.

Key Concept 8.4

If we really take seriously the idea that doing integration well involves loving God and neighbor, then our Christian faith will shape our work within psychology to be oriented toward love and justice.

As we consider the embodied components of integration, there is always some degree of human agency involved in working for justice, and God desires that we practice love and justice within neighborhoods, communities, and the wider society. For some, work within psychotherapy can be seen as a form of working toward justice, as we may work with clients or patients that have internalized racism, or have encountered racialized, intergenerational, and other forms of trauma due to oppression or marginalization. In addition to this, we must be careful to work to understand our own racial identity, and the racialized dynamics that could exclude and oppress others. We must also become more aware of any privileges that pertain to our own racial identity. All of this is also part of practicing integration well.

As we think about the future of integration, one of our primary interests is to empower you as students and professionals within the field of psychology to know that your contribution to integration is valuable, unique, and essential to shape the integration dialogue in the years to come. Raising up a generation of multicultural integrators who think deeply about their faith, speak from their own theological and cultural location, are transformed by God's Spirit, and work toward greater love and justice, is what the future of integration will look like. Finding your voice in the integration dialogue means that you continue to reflect on your faith, cultural identity, and interests in psychology, and that you begin to let yourself be changed by God's Spirit in the process. While this is an important first step, it doesn't stop there. Finding your voice means that we also work to share and speak about our integrative reflections and identity, and then let this integrative vision shape our vocations. As authors, we want you to feel empowered to bring your own cultural and faith stories into your studies in psychology in such a way that works toward greater love and justice. We hope that you will continue to share your integrative reflections and identity, write about it in papers, publish in journals, present at conferences, and in so doing expand the field of integration.

Wrapping Things Up

As we close, we invite you to continue to develop your own integrative reflections and integrative identity. These movements of developing our views and practices of integration are part of learning to love and understand God, others, and yourself, and involve a tangible way that you can extend love and work for justice. We invite you to live out this aspect of your integrative identity in your day-to-day life in the context where God has placed you. Donald Miller captures how change and growth also involve possibility and invitation. As we close, consider these words from Miller's (2005) *Through Painted Deserts: Light, God, and Beauty on the Open Road*:

> So my prayer is that your story will have involved some leaving and some coming home, some summer and some winter, some roses blooming out like children in a play. My hope is your story will be about changing, about getting something beautiful born inside of you, about learning to love . . . about moving yourself around water, around mountains, around friends, about learning to love others more than we love ourselves, about learning oneness as a way of understanding God. We get one story, you and I, and one story alone. God has established the elements, the setting and the climax and the resolution. It would be a crime not to venture out, wouldn't it?

As we have traveled through this integration journey with you, we hope that you have discovered something new about loving God, others, and yourself in this process. Our hope and prayer is that you will continue to use your training in psychology to create spaces for others to experience God's love, justice, and restoration.

Final Reflection Questions

1. Recall and identify your particular religious/spiritual or denominational background from chapter two. How did the religious/ spiritual messages shape your own particular views of psychology? What were the messages given to you by your religious/ spiritual background about your vocation?

2. What messages were given in your religious/spiritual background about how one finds healing? Do any of these themes overlap or conflict with psychology? How?

3. Review Hay's ADDRESSING model and remind yourself of these aspects of your identity. In what ways was Hays's ADDRESSING model helpful for you in understanding messages about your own cultural identity? How might the discipline of psychology inform or broaden these aspects of your identity? How might your Christian faith inform or broaden aspects of this identity?

4. Think back to the cultural and family stories that have positively impacted you. Write down several of these or share them with a friend. Offer a prayer of thanks for strengths and resources in your cultural and family stories that you've identified.

5. Think back to spiritual mentors or church communities that have positively impacted you. Write down several of these or share them with a friend. Offer a prayer of thanks for strengths and resources from these mentors or church communities that you've identified.

6. Think about the particular context where you currently are. What ways might you be able to extend love and work for justice? How have your views changed on this after reading this chapter?

7. Pray and ask for the next steps on how you might extend love and work for justice within the particular context where you are situated. What might these be? What ideas, thoughts, or feelings come up as you reflect on your vocation and extending love and working toward justice?

8. What were some themes from this chapter that God spoke to you about? How have your views about vocation changed? What was helpful? What was most challenging?

Bibliography

Abernethy, A. D. (2012). Integration: Toward a variety of musical ensembles. *Journal of Psychology and Theology*, *40*(2), 122-26. https://doi.org/10.1177/009164711204000207

Abernethy, A. D., Houston, T. R., Mimms, T., & Boyd-Franklin, N. (2006). Using prayer in psychotherapy: Applying Sue's differential to enhance culturally competent care. *Cultural Diversity & Ethnic Minority Psychology*, *12*, 101-14. http://dx.doi.org/10.1037/1099-9809.12.1.101

Achtemeier, P. J., & Boraas, R. S. (1996). Know, Knowledge. In *The HarperCollins Bible Dictionary*. HarperOne.

Adames, H. Y., Chavez-Dueñas, N. Y., Sharma, S., & La Roche, M. J. (2018). Intersectionality in psychotherapy: The experiences of an AfroLatinx queer immigrant. *Psychotherapy*, *55*(1), 73-79. https://doi.org/10.1037/pst0000152

Adichie, C. N. (2009). *The danger of a single story* [Video]. TED Conferences. http://www.ted.com/talks/chimamanda_adichie_the_danger_of_a_single_story

Allport, G. W., & Ross, J. M. (1967). Personal religious orientation and prejudice. *Journal of Personality & Social Psychology*, *5*(4), 432-43. https://doi.org/10.1037/0022-3514.5.4.432

An, C. H., West, A. D., Sandage, S. J., & Bell, C. A. (2019). Relational spirituality, mature alterity, and spiritual service among ministry leaders: An empirical study. *Pastoral Psychology*, *68*(2), 127-43. https://doi.org/10.1007/s11089-018-0846-9

An, S. (2020). Disrupting curriculum of violence on Asian Americans. *Review of Education, Pedagogy, and Cultural Studies*, *42*(2), 141-56.

Antonio, E. P. (2011). Black theology. In I. A. McFarland, D. A. S. Fergusson, K. Kilby & I. R. Torrance, (Eds.), *Cambridge dictionary of Christian theology* (pp. 51-76). Cambridge University Press.

APA. (2002). *Guidelines on multicultural education, training, research, practice, and organizational change for psychologists*. Author.

APA. (2017). *Multicultural guidelines: An ecological approach to context, identity, and intersectionality*. http://www.apa.org/about/policy/multicultural-guidelines.pdf

Aquino, M. P. (1993). *Our cry for life: Feminist theology from Latin America*. Orbis Books.

Aquino, M. P., Machado, D. L., & Rodriguez, J. (2002). *A reader in Latina feminist theology: Religion and justice* (1st ed.). University of Texas Press.

Armstrong, T. R., Wangugi, A., & Scott, S. N. (2022). Unpacking of a legacy: Womanist theology and clinical implications. *Journal of Psychology and Theology*, *50*(1), 63-72. https://doi.org/10.1177/00916471211071060

Attanasio, C. (2020, April 26). El Paso Walmart shooting victim dies, death toll now 23. *The Seattle Times*. https://www.seattletimes.com/business/el-paso-shooting-victim -dies-months-later-death-toll-now-23/

Bacote, V. (2020). *Reckoning with race and performing the good news: In search of a better evangelical theology*. Brill.

Banks, M. E., & Lee, S. (2016). Womanism and spirituality/theology. In T. Bryant-Davis, & L. Comas-Díaz (Eds.), *Womanist and mujerista psychologies: Voices of fire, acts of courage* (pp. 123-48). APA. http://www.doi.org/10.1037/14937-006

Barclay, W. (1976). *The letters of James and Peter*. Westminster.

Barndt, J. (2011). *Becoming an anti-racist church: Journeying toward wholeness*. Fortress.

Barth, K. (1961). *Church dogmatics*, Vol. 2, (G. W. Bromiley, Trans.; G. W. Bromiley & T. F. Torrance, Eds.). T&T Clark.

Barth, K. (1981). *Letters, 1961–1968*. (G. W. Bromiley, Trans.; J. Fangmeier & H. Stoevesandt, Eds.). Eerdmans.

BBC. (2021, March 22). Atlanta spa shootings: Who are the victims? https://www.bbc .com/news/world-us-canada-56446771

BBC. (2021, May 21). Covid "hate crimes" against Asian Americans on rise. https://www .bbc.com/news/world-us-canada-56218684

Beed, C., & Beed, C. (2015). Social sin, theology and social science. *Journal of Catholic Social Thought, 12*(2), 279-300.

Bering, J. M. (2012). *The belief instinct: The psychology of souls, destiny, and the meaning of life*. W. W. Norton.

Billings, T. J. (2016). How learning to lament can help fight racism. *Relevant Magazine*. https://www.relevantmagazine.com/current/how-learning-lament-can -help-fight-racism/

Blozis, S. A. (2012). *Nonlinear growth modeling*. In B. Laursen, T. D. Little, & N. A. Card (Eds.), *Handbook of developmental research methods* (pp. 445-63). Guilford.

Bookman-Zandler, R., & Smith, J. M. (2023). Healing the collective: Community-healing models and the complex relationship between individual trauma and historical trauma in First Nations survivors. *Journal of Psychology and Theology*. Advanced online publication. https://doi.org/10.1177/00916471221149101

Bowker, J. (1998). Science and religion: Contest or confirmation. In F. Watts (Ed.) *Science meets faith* (pp. 95-119). SPCK.

Brown B. (2012). *Daring greatly: How the courage to be vulnerable transforms the way we live, love, parent, and lead*. Gotham Books.

Brown, R. M. A. (1984). *Unexpected news: Reading the Bible with third world eyes*. Westminster.

Brown, W. S., & Strawn, B. D. (2012). *The physical nature of Christian life: Neuroscience, psychology, and the church.* Cambridge University Press.

Brueggemann, W. (1986). The costly loss of lament. *Journal for the Study of the Old Testament, 11*(36), 57-71.

Brueggemann, W. (1995). *The psalms and the life of faith.* Fortress.

Brueggemann, W. (2016). *God, neighbor, empire: The excess of divine fidelity and the command of common good.* Baylor University Press.

Bryant-Davis, T. (2020). *Wisdom from Womanist Psychology: Integrating art, spirit, activism, and community* [Conference Lecture]. Fuller Dialogues. https://fullerstudio .fuller.edu/fuller-dialogues-holistic-healing-and-wellness/

Bryant-Davis, T., Ellis, M. T., & Perez, B. (2013). Women of color and spirituality: Faith to move mountains. In L. Comas-Díaz & B. Greene (Eds.), *Psychological health of women of color: Inter-sections, challenges, and opportunities* (pp. 303-15). Praeger.

Burns, J. W., Quartana, P., Gilliam, W., Gray, E., Matsuura, J., Nappi, C., Wolfe, B., & Lofland, K. (2008). Effects of anger suppression on pain severity and pain behaviors among chronic pain patients: Evaluation of an ironic process model. *Health Psychology, 27*(5), 645-52. https://doi.org/10.1037/a0013044

Cahill, L. S. (2013). *Global justice, Christology and Christian ethics.* Cambridge University Press.

Callaway, K., & Whitney, W. B. (2022). *Theology for psychology and counseling: An invitation to holistic Christian practice.* Baker Academic.

Calvin, J. (1960). *Institutes of the Christian religion, vol. 1.* (J. T. McNeill, Ed.; F. L. Battles, Trans.). Westminster.

Carel, H. H., & Kidd, I. J. (2014). Epistemic injustice in healthcare: A philosophical analysis. *Medicine, Health Care and Philosophy, 17*(4), 529-540. https://doi.org /10.1007/s11019-014-9560-2

Carter, J. K. (2008). *Race: A theological account.* Oxford University Press.

CBS SF Bay Area. (2021, March 15). Second suspect arrested in fatal Oakland assault, robbery of 75-year-old Asian man. https://sanfrancisco.cbslocal.com/2021/03/15/second -suspect-arrested-fatal-oakland-assault-robbery-75-year-old-asian-man-pak-ho/

Chalfant, P., Heller, P., Roberts, A., Briones, D., Aguirre-Hochbaum, S., & Fan, W. (1990). The clergy as a resource for those encountering psychological distress. *Review of Religious Research, 31*(2), 305-17.

ChenFeng, J. (2018a). Integration of self and family: Asian American Christians in the midst of White evangelicalism and being the model minority. In E. E. Wilson & L. Nice (Eds.), *Socially just religious and spiritual interventions: AFTA SpringerBriefs in family therapy.* https://doi.org/10.1007/978-3-030-01986-0_2

ChenFeng J. (2018b). *Relational wellness for second generation Asian American adult children.* Presentation at the California State University, Northridge, Northridge, CA, United States.

Coe, J. H., & Hall, T. W. (2010). *Psychology in the Spirit: Contours of a transformational psychology.* InterVarsity Press.

Cohen, A. B., & Hill, P. C. (2007). Religion as culture: Religious individualism and collectivism among American Catholics, Jews, and Protestants. *Journal of Personality, 75*(4), 709-42. https://doi.org/10.1111/j.1467-6494.2007.00454.x

Comas-Díaz, L. (2011). *Multicultural care: A clinician's guide to cultural competence.* APA.

Comas-Díaz, L. (2016). Mujerista psychospirituality. In T. Bryant-Davis & L. Comas-Díaz (Eds.), *Womanist and mujerista psychologies: Voices of fire, acts of courage* (pp. 149-69). APA. https://doi.org/10.1037/14937-007

Cone, J. H. (1970). *A Black theology of liberation.* J. B. Lippincott.

Cone, J. H. (2011). *The cross and the lynching tree.* Orbis.

Cone, J. H. (2012a). *God of the oppressed.* Orbis.

Cone, J. H. (2012b). Theology's great sin: Silence in the face of white supremacy. In D. Hopkins & E. Antonio (Eds.), *The Cambridge Companion to Black Theology* (pp. 143-55). Cambridge University Press.

Cooper-White, P. (2014, April 19). *Holy Saturday* [Homily]. Holy Trinity Parish (Episcopal), Decatur, GA.

Corasaniti, N., Pérez-Peña, R., & Alvarez, L. (2015, June 18). Church massacre suspect held as Charleston grieves. *The New York Times.* https://www.nytimes.com/2015/06/19/us/charleston-church-shooting.html

Crabtree, K. (2021, May 24). How racially targeted mass shootings can alter community politics. *The Washington Post.* https://www.washingtonpost.com/politics/2021/05/24/how-racially-targeted-mass-shootings-can-alter-community-politics/

Crenshaw, K. (1989). Demarginalizing the intersection of race and sex: A Black feminist critique of antidiscrimination doctrine, feminist theory and antiracist politics. *University of Chicago Legal Forum, 1.* https://chicagounbound.uchicago.edu/uclf/vol1989/iss1/8/?utm_source=chicagounbound.uchicago.edu%2Fuclf%2Fvol1989%2Fiss1%2F8&utm_medium=PDF&utm_campaign=PDFCoverPages

Cuddy, A. (2012). *Your body language may shape who you are* [Video]. TED Conferences. https://www.ted.com/talks/amy_cuddy_your_body_language_shapes_who_you_are/up-next?language=en

Deddo, G. (1997). Persons in racial reconciliation: The contributions of a Trinitarian theological anthropology. In L. Okholm (Ed.), *The gospel in Black and White: Theological resources for racial reconciliation* (pp. 58-70). InterVarsity Press.

Deffler, S. A., Leary, M. R., & Hoyle, R. H. (2016). Knowing what you know: Intellectual humility and judgments of recognition memory. *Personality and Individual Differences, 96*, 255-59. https://doi.org/10.1016/j.paid.2016.03.016

Dictionary.com. (n.d.). Liminal. In Dictionary.com. Retrieved July 13, 2021, from https://www.dictionary.com/browse/liminal

Dwiwardani, C., & Whitney, W. B. (2022). The cycle of cultural integration: Toward hermeneutical justice in the integration of psychology and theology. *Journal of Psychology and Theology.* Advanced online publication. https://doi.org/10.1177/00916471221130333

Dyrness, W. (1997). *The earth is God's: A theology of American culture.* Orbis Books.

Ecklund, E. H., Johnson, D. R., Vaidyanathan, B., Matthews, K. R. W., Lewis, S. W., Thomson, R. A., Jr., & Di, D. (2019). *Secularity and science: What scientists around the world really think about religion.* Oxford University Press.

Ecklund, K. (2016). *Cultural psychology & Christian diversity: Developing cultural competence for a diverse Christian community.* Abilene Christian University Press.

Entwistle, D. N. (2015). *Integrative approaches to psychology and Christianity: An introduction to worldview issues, philosophical foundations, and models of integration* (3rd ed.). Cascade Books.

Erikson, E. (1963). *Childhood and society.* W. W. Norton.

Eriksson, C. B., & Abernethy, A. D. (2014). Integration in multicultural competence and diversity training: Engaging difference and grace. *Journal of Psychology and Theology, 42*(2), 174-87.

Evans, R. B. (1999). A century of psychology. *APA Monitor, 30*(10), 14-30.

Farrow, D. (1995). St. Irenaeus of Lyons: The church and the world. *Pro Ecclesia, 4,* 348-65.

Flemming, D. (2005). *Contextualization in the New Testament: Patterns for theology and mission.* InterVarsity Press.

Freud, S. (1961). The future of an illusion. In J. Strachey (Ed. & Trans.), *The standard edition of the complete psychological works of Sigmund Freud* (Vol. 21, pp. 5-56). Hogarth.

Fricker, M. (2007). *Epistemic injustice: Power and the ethics of knowing.* Oxford University Press.

Gadamer, H. G. (1975). *Truth and method.* Seabury.

Gaebelein, F. (1954). *The pattern of God's truth: The integration of faith and learning.* Oxford University Press.

Garzon, F., & Tan, S. (1992). Counseling Hispanics: Cross-cultural and Christian perspectives. *Journal of Psychology and Christianity, 11*(4), 378-90.

Goldingay, J. (2019). *Old Testament ethics: A guided tour.* IVP Academic.

Graham, S., Munniksma, A., & Juvonen, J. (2014). Psychosocial benefits of cross-ethnic friendships in urban middle schools. *Child Development, 85,* 469-83.

Green, J. B. (1997). *New international commentary on the New Testament: Luke.* Eerdmans.

Green, J. B. (2008). *Body, soul, and human life: The nature of humanity in the Bible.* Baker Academic.

Gregg, A. P., & Mahadevan, N. (2014). Intellectual arrogance and intellectual humility: An evolutionary-epistemological account. *Journal of Psychology and Theology, 42*(1), 7-18. https://doi.org/10.1177/009164711404200102

Grenz, S. J. (2000). *Theology for the community of God.* Eerdmans.

Gunton, C. E. (2003). *Father, son and holy spirit.* T&T Clark.

Gunton, C. E. (2004). *The Christian faith: An introduction to Christian doctrine.* Blackwell.

Gunton, C. E. (2005). *The one, the three and the many: God, creation and the culture of modernity.* Cambridge University Press.

Gushee, D. P. (2013). *The sacredness of human life: Why an ancient biblical vision is key to the world's future*. Eerdmans.

Hall, E. T. (1976). *Beyond culture*. Anchor.

Hall, M. E. L. (2010). Confessions of a tortoise: Slow steps on the integration journey. In G. Moriarty (Ed.), *Integrating faith and psychology: Twelve psychologists tell their stories* (pp. 111-32). InterVarsity Press.

Hall, M. E. L. (2016). Suffering in God's presence: The role of lament in transformation. *Journal of Spiritual Formation and Soul Care, 9*, 219-32.

Harper, L. S. (2016). *The very good gospel: How everything wrong can be made right*. WaterBrook.

Harris, A. L. (2020). *Is Christianity the White man's religion? How the Bible is good news for people of color*. InterVarsity Press.

Hathaway, W. L., & Yarhouse, M. A. (2021). *The integration of psychology and Christianity: A domain-based approach*. InterVarsity Press.

Hays, P. A. (2008). *Addressing cultural complexities in practice, second edition: Assessment, diagnosis, and therapy*. APA.

Hoard, P., & Hoard, B. (2023). Eucontamination: Enacting a centered-set theology in a multicultural world. *Journal of Psychology and Theology*. Advanced online publication. https://doi.org/10.1177/00916471231173201

Holmes, A. F. (1975). *The idea of a Christian college*. Eerdmans.

Hook, J., Zuniga, S., Wang, D., Brown, E. M., Dwiwardani, C., & Sandage, S. J. (2023). Conviction, competence, context: A three-level model to promote racial diversity, equity, and inclusion among Christians. *Journal of Psychology and Christianity, 42*(2), 97-115.

Hook, J. N., & Davis, D. E. (2012). Integration, multicultural counseling, and social justice. *Journal of Psychology and Theology, 40*(2), 102.

Houston-Armstrong, T., & Callaway. K. (2023). The beautiful mess of collaboration: An embodied pedagogy for teaching across disciplines, genders, races and theological traditions. *Journal of Psychology and Christianity, 42*, 51-58.

Hunt, L. M. (2001). Beyond cultural competence: Applying humility to clinical settings. *Religiously Informed Cultural Competence, 24*, 134-36.

Isasi-Díaz, A. M. (1996). *Mujerista theology: A theology for the twenty-first century*. Orbis Books.

Javier, R. A. (2007). *The bilingual mind: Thinking, feeling, and speaking in two languages*. New York: Springer.

Jenkins, P. (2011). *The next Christendom: The coming of global Christianity*. Oxford University Press.

Jinkins, M. (2015). *Invitation to theology: A guide to study, conversation & practice*. InterVarsity Press.

Johnson, E. L. (Ed.). (2010). *Psychology and Christianity: Five views*. IVP Academic.

Johnston, R. K. (2014). *God's wider presence: Reconsidering general revelation*. Baker Academic.

Jones, H., Kallimel, G., Stephens, R., & Wang, D. (2023). Black liberation integrative psychology: Implications for clinical theory and practice. *Journal of Psychology and Theology*. Advanced online publication. https://doi.org/10.1177/00916471221149108

Jones, R. P. (2020). *White too long: The legacy of White supremacy in American Christianity*. Simon & Schuster.

Jun, A., Jones Jolivet, T. L., Ash, A. N., & Collins, C. S. (2018). *White Jesus: The architecture of racism in religion and education*. Peter Lang.

Kamara, D. (2021, September 29). Opinion: Latinx vs. Latine. *The Tulane Hullabaloo*. https://tulanehullabaloo.com/57213/intersections/opinion-latinx-vs-latine/

Kärkkäinen, V. M. (2018). *Pneumatology: The Holy Spirit in ecumenical, international, and contextual perspective*. Baker Academic.

Katongole, E., & Rice, C. (2008). *Reconciling all things: A Christian vision for justice, peace and healing*. InterVarsity Press.

Keener, C. S. (2011). *Miracles: The Credibility of the New Testament accounts*. Vol. 1. Baker.

Kierkegaard, S. (1995). *Søren Kierkegaard's journals and papers*. H. Hong, Trans. InteLex.

Kim, G. J.-S., & Shaw, S. M. (2018). *Intersectional theology: An introductory guide*. Fortress.

Kim, N. (2007). The "indigestible" Asian: The unifying term "Asian" in theological discourse. In R. N. Brock (Ed.), *Off the menu: Asian and Asian North American women's religion and theology* (1st ed.). Westminster John Knox.

Kim, P. Y., Locke, M. A., Shakil, E., Lee, J.-H., & Chiangpradit, N. V. (2023). Beliefs about Jesus's race, implicit bias, and cultural correlates among Asian American college students. *Journal of Psychology and Theology*. Advanced online publication. https://doi.org/10.1177/00916471231161585

Kim-Kort, M. (2012). *Making paper cranes: Toward an Asian American feminist theology*. Chalice.

King, M. L., Jr. (1963). *Letter from Birmingham jail*. Beacon.

King, M. L., Jr. (2019). *Strength to Love*. Beacon.

King, P. E., & Whitney, W. (2015). What's the "positive" in positive psychology? Teleological considerations of the doctrine of creation and the imago dei. *Journal of Psychology and Theology, 43*, 47-59.

Kuyper, A. (1961). *Lectures on Calvinism*. Eerdmans.

Labberton, M. (2014). *Called: The crisis and promise of following Jesus today*. InterVarsity Press.

Lee, D. D. (2022). *Doing Asian American theology: A contextual framework for faith and practice*. IVP Academic.

Leung, S. (2021, April 17). Elderly Asian Americans are living in fear as assaults, confrontations soar. A retiree worries: "If people beat me, I can die right away." *Boston Globe*. https://www.bostonglobe.com/2021/04/17/metro/elderly-asian-americans-are-living-fear-assaults-confrontations-soar-retiree-worries-if-people-beat-me-i-can-die-right-away/

Lewis, C. S. (2009). *The magician's nephew*. HarperCollins.

Lewis, C. S. (2012). *Mere Christianity*. William Collins.

MacIntyre, A. (2007). *After virtue: A study in moral theory* (3rd ed.). University of Notre Dame Press.

Mafico, T. L. (1992). Just, Justice. In *The Anchor Yale Bible Dictionary: H-J* (pp. 1127-29). Yale University Press.

Manickam, J. A. (2008). Race, racism and ethnicity. In W. A. Dyrness & V. M. Kärkkäinen (Eds.), *Global dictionary of theology*. InterVarsity Press.

Marshall, C. D. (2012). Divine justice as restorative justice. In R. B. Kruschwitz (Ed.), *Prison: Christian Reflection Series on Faith and Ethics*. Baylor Center for Christian Ethics. https://www.baylor.edu/content/services/document.php/163072.pdf

Marshall, C. D., Swartley, W. M., & Noakes-Duncan, T. M. I. (2018). *All things reconciled: Essays in restorative justice, religious violence, and the interpretation of Scripture*. Cascade Books.

Martell-Otero, L. I., Pérez, Z. M., Conde-Frazier, E., & Jones, S. (2013). *Latina evangélicas: A theological survey from the margins*. Cascade Books.

Martin, J. (2012). *The Jesuit guide to (almost) everything*. HarperOne.

McBeth, L. (1987). *The Baptist heritage*. Broadman.

McClendon, J. W. (1974). *Biography as theology*. Abingdon.

McConnell, J. M., Bacote, V., Davis, E. B., Brown, E. M., Fort, C. J., Liu, T., Worthington, E. L., Hook, J. N., & Davis, D. E. (2021a). Including multiculturalism, social justice, and peace within the integration of psychology and theology: Barriers and a call to action. *Journal of Psychology and Theology, 49*(1), 5-21. https://doi.org/10.1177/0091647120974989

McConnell, J. M., Liu, T., Brown, E. M., Fort, C. J., Azcuna, D. R., Tabiolo, C. A. M., Kibble, C. D. M., & Winslow, A. B. (2021b). The multicultural peace and justice collaborative: Critical peace education in a research training environment. *Peace and Conflict: Journal of Peace Psychology, 27*(2), 191-202. https://doi.org/10.1037/pac0000539

McIntosh, P. (2003). White privilege: Unpacking the invisible knapsack. In S. Plous (Ed.), *Understanding prejudice and discrimination* (pp. 191-96). McGraw-Hill.

McKnight, S. (2018). *The blue parakeet: Rethinking how you read the Bible*. Zondervan.

McNeil, J. D. (2010). Reluctant integration. In G. Moriarty (Ed.), *Integrating faith and psychology: Twelve psychologists tell their stories* (pp. 188-208). InterVarsity Press.

McNeil, J. D., & Pozzi, C. (2007). Developing multicultural competency. In R. J. Priest & A. L. Nieves (Eds.), *This side of heaven: Race, ethnicity, and Christian faith* (pp. 81-94). Oxford University Press.

McWilliams, N. (2011). *Psychoanalytic diagnosis: Understanding personality structure in the clinical process* (2nd ed.). Guilford.

Menges, R., & Exum, W. (1983). Barriers to the progress of women and minority faculty. *The Journal of Higher Education, 54*(2), 123-44. doi:10.2307/1981567

Merritt, J. (2013, December 12). Insisting Jesus was White is bad history and bad theology. *Atlantic Monthly.* http://www.theatlantic.com/politics/archive/2013/12/insisting-jesus -was-white-is-bad-history-and-bad-theology/282310/

Migliore, D. L. (2004). *Faith seeking understanding: An introduction to Christian theology* (3rd ed.). Eerdmans.

Miller, D. (2005). *Through painted deserts: Light, God, and beauty on the open road.* Thomas Nelson.

Mirecki, P. (2000). Gnosticism. In D. N. Freedman, A. B. Beck, & A. C. Myers (Eds.), *Eerdmans Dictionary of the Bible* (pp. 507-9). Eerdmans.

Moltmann, J. (1985). *God in creation: A new theology of creation and the spirit of God.* Fortress.

Moltmann, J. (1993). *The crucified God.* Fortress.

Moltmann, J. (1997). *The source of life: The holy spirit and the theology of life.* Fortress.

Moreno, O., & Cardemil, E. (2018). Religiosity and well-being among Mexican-born and US-born Mexicans: A qualitative investigation. *Journal of Latina/o Psychology, 6*(3), 235-47. https://doi.org/10.1037/lat0000099

Murphy, N. (2018). *A philosophy of the Christian religion.* SPCK.

Muthiah, R. (2021, January 12). The theological work of antiracism needs to include lament. *The Christian Century.* https://www.christiancentury.org/article/critical -essay/theological-work-antiracism-needs-include-lament

Myers, D. G., & DeWall, C. N. (2018). *Psychology* (12th ed.). Worth.

Neason, A. (2020, May 20). Ahmaud Arbery, Breonna Taylor and covering Black deaths. *Columbia Journalism Review.* https://www.cjr.org/criticism/ahmaud-arbery-breonna -taylor.php

Neff, M. A., & McMinn, M. R. (2020). *Embodying integration: A fresh look at Christianity in the therapy room.* InterVarsity Press.

Noll, M. A. (1998). The Bible and slavery. In R. M. Miller, H. S. Stout, & C. W. Wilson (Eds.), *Religion and the American Civil War* (pp. 43-73). Oxford University Press.

Noll, M. A. (2019). *A History of Christianity in the United States and Canada.* Eerdmans.

Padgett, G. (2015). A critical case study of selected U.S. history textbooks from a tribal critical race theory perspective. *The Qualitative Report, 20*(3), 153-71. https://doi .org/10.46743/2160-3715/ 2015.2106

Pak, J. H., Che, H., Chung, E., Dolores, A., Baronia, A., & Schupanizt, T. (2023). Decolonizing psychology and integrating a critical hermeneutic framework to heal racial disunity in faith-based clinical programs. *Journal of Psychology and Christianity, 42*(2), 127-43.

Park, C. L. (2010). Making sense of the meaning literature: An integrative review of meaning making and its effects on adjustment to stressful life events. *Psychological Bulletin, 136*(2), 257-301. https://doi.org/10.1037/a0018301

Pederson, P. (1990). The multicultural perspective as a fourth force in counseling. *Journal of Mental Health Counseling, 12,* 93-95.

Pettigrew, T. (1998). Intergroup contact theory. *Annual Review of Psychology, 49,* 65-85.

Pew Research Center. (n.d.). *Religious landscape study: Latinos.* Retrieved July 8, 2021, from https://www.pewforum.org/religious-landscape-study/racial-and-ethnic-composition/latino/

Pew Research Center. (2013). *The rise of Asian Americans.* https://www.pewresearch.org/social-trends/wp-content/uploads/sites/3/2013/04/Asian-Americans-new-full-report-04-2013.pdf

Pew Research Center. (2015). *U.S. public becoming less religious: Modest drop in overall rates of belief and practice, but religiously affiliated Americans are as observant as before.* https://www.pewforum.org/wp-content/uploads/sites/7/2015/11/201.11.03_RLS_II_full_report.pdf

Pew Research Center. (2018, February). *5 facts about the religious lives of African Americans.* https://www.pewresearch.org/fact-tank/2018/02/07/5-facts-about-the-religious-lives-of-african-americans/

Pew Research Center. (2018, April). *Black Americans are more likely than overall public to be Christian, Protestant.* https://www.pewresearch.org/fact-tank/2018/04/23/black-americans-are-more-likely-than-overall-public-to-be-christian-protestant/

Pew Research Forum. (2019). *Seven facts about Southern Baptists.* Pew Research Center. https://www.pewresearch.org/fact-tank/2019/06/07/7-facts-about-southern-baptists/

Plantinga, C. (2002). *Engaging God's world: A Christian vision of faith, learning, and living.* Eerdmans.

Rah, S.-C. (2015). *Prophetic lament: A challenge to the Western church.* InterVarsity Press.

Roberton, T., Daffern, M., & Bucks, R. S. (2015). Beyond anger control: Difficulty attending to emotions also predicts aggression in offenders. *Psychology of Violence, 5*(1), 74-83. https://doi.org/10.1037/a0037214

Roberts, W. L. (1986). Nonlinear models of development: An example from the socialization of competence. *Child Development, 57*(5), 1166-78. doi:10.2307/1130440.

Rohr, R. (1999). *Everything belongs: The gift of contemplative prayer.* Crossroad.

Romero, R. C., & Liou, J. M. (2023). *Christianity and critical race theory: A faithful and constructive conversation.* Baker Academic.

Sandage, S. J., & Brown, J. K. (2018). *Relational integration of psychology and Christian theology: Theory, research, practice.* Routledge.

Sandage, S. J., & Harden, M. G. (2011). Relational spirituality, a differentiation of self, and virtue as predictors of intercultural development. *Mental Health, Religion & Culture, 14*(8), 819-38. https://doi.org/10.1080/13674676.2010.527932

Selasi, T. (2014). *Don't ask where I am from, ask where I am a local* [Video]. TED Conferences. https://www.ted.com/talks/taiye_selasi_don_t_ask_where_i_m_from_ask_where_i_m_a_local?language=en

Shelton, A. J., & Dwiwardani, C. (2022). Multiculturalism and diversity in integration journals: A content analysis of JPT and JPC, 1973–2020. *Journal of Psychology and Theology.* Advanced online publication. https://doi.org/10.1177/00916471221126153

Shields, S. A. (2008). Gender: An intersectionality perspective. *Sex Roles, 59,* 301-11.

Shim, H. (2017, August 22). Questions on (the limits & effects of) Asian American allyship. *Medium.* https://medium.com/@persimmontree/questions-on-the-limits -effects-of-asian-american-allyship-bb545f019117

Simundson, D. J. (1989). Mental health in the Bible. *Word & World, 9*(2), 140-46.

Smith, C. (2003). *Moral, believing animals: Human personhood and culture.* Oxford University Press.

Smith, H. (2021, May 21). Anti-Asian hate crimes have spiked in cities around the U.S., study finds. *Los Angeles Times.* https://www.latimes.com/california/story/2021-05-04 /anti-asian-hate-crimes-spike-us-cities-study-finds/

Smith, J. K. A. (2009). *Desiring the kingdom: Worship, worldview, and cultural formation.* Baker Academic.

Smith, J. K. A. (2016). *You are what you love: The spiritual power of habit.* Brazos.

Southern Seminary Special Report: Racism and the History of Slavery (2018). The Southern Baptist Theological Seminary. https://sbts-wordpress-uploads.s3.amazonaws.com /sbts/uploads/2018/12/Racism-and-the-Legacy-of-Slavery-Report-v3.pdf

Steger, M. F., & Park, C. L. (2012). The creation of meaning following trauma: Meaning making and trajectories of distress and recovery. In R. A. McMackin, E. Newman, J. M. Fogler, & T. M. Keane (Eds.), *Trauma therapy in context: The science and craft of evidence-based practice* (pp. 171-91). APA Books.

Stone, H. W., & Duke, J. O. (2013). *How to think theologically* (3rd ed.). Fortress.

Strahan, J. M. (2012). *The limits of a text: Luke 23:34a as a case study in theological interpretation.* Penn State University Press.

Strawn, B. D. (n.d.). *Integration: With what and with whom?* Fuller Studio. Retrieved July 12, 2023, from https://fullerstudio.fuller.edu/integration-what-with-what -and-with-whom/

Strawn, B. D., Bland, E. D., & Flores, P. S. (2018). Learning clinical integration: A case study approach. *Journal of Psychology and Theology, 46*(2), 85-97. https://doi.org /10.1177/0091647118767976

Strawn, B. D., Wright, R. W., & Jones, P. (2014). Tradition-based integration: Illuminating the stories and practices that shape our integrative imaginations. *Journal of Psychology and Christianity, 33*(4), 300.

Tan, J. Y. (2008). *Introducing Asian American Theologies.* Orbis Books.

Tan, S.-Y., & Dong, N. J. (2014). Psychotherapy with members of Asian-American churches and spiritual traditions. In P. S. Richards & A. E. Bergin (Eds.), *Handbook of psychotherapy and religious diversity* (p. 423-50). APA. https://doi.org/10.1037 /14371-017

Tanner, K. (2010a). *Christ the key*. Cambridge University Press.

Tanner, K. (2010b). Christian claims: How my mind has changed. *The Christian Century, 127*(4), 41-46.

Taylor, C. (1989). *Sources of the self: The making of the modern identity*. Harvard University Press.

Tedeschi, R. G., Park, C. L., & Calhoun, L. G. (1998). *Posttraumatic growth: Positive changes in the aftermath of crisis*. Erlbaum.

Tervalon, M., & Murray-Garcia, J. (1998). Cultural humility versus cultural competence: A critical distinction in defining physician training outcomes in multicultural education. *Journal of Health Care for the Poor and Underserved, 9*(2), 117-25. https://www.doi.org/10.1353/hpu.2010.0233

Thurman, H. (1996). *Jesus and the disinherited*. Beacon.

Turner, V. (1974). Liminal to liminoid in play, flow, and ritual: An essay in comparative symbology. *Rice University Studies, 60*(3), 53-92.

Twiss, R. (2015). *Rescuing the gospel from the cowboys: A Native American expression of the Jesus way*. InterVarsity Press.

Tyson, P. J., Jones, D., & Elcock, J. (2011). *Psychology in social context: Issues and debate*. Blackwell.

Unidos US & John Hopkins School of Education. (2023). *Analyzing inclusion of Latino contributions in U.S. history curriculum for high school*. https://unidosus.org/wp-content/uploads/2023/05/unidosus_johnshopkins_analyzinginclusionoflatinocontributionsinushistorycurriculaforhighschools.pdf

U.S. Census Bureau (n. d.). Race. Retrieved July 23, 2019, from https://www.census.gov/quickfacts/fact/note/US/RHI625218

van der Kolk, B. A. (2014). *The body keeps the score: Brain, mind, and body in the healing of trauma*. Viking.

Villodas, R. A., Jr. (2020). *The deeply formed life: Five transformative values to root us in the way of Jesus*. WaterBrook.

Volf, M. (2019). *Exclusion & embrace: A theological exploration of identity, otherness, and reconciliation* (Rev. ed.). Abingdon.

Volf, M., & Croasmun, M. (2021). *For the life of the world: Theology that makes a difference*. Brazos.

Wang, P. S., Berglund, P. A., & Kessler, R. C. (2003). Patterns and correlates of contacting clergy for mental disorders in the United States. *Health Services Research, 38*(2), 647-73. https://doi.org/10.1111/14756773.00138

Ware, L. (2000). People of color in the academy: Patterns of discrimination in faculty hiring and retention. *Boston College Third World Law Journal, 20*(1), 55-76. http://heinonline.org/HOL/Page?handle=hein.journals/bctw20&div=10&g_sent=1&casa_token= &collection=journals

Webster, J. (2003). The human person. In K. J. Vanhoozer (Ed.), *The Cambridge companion to postmodern theology* (pp. 219-34). Cambridge University Press.

Whitney, W. B. (2020). Beginnings: Why the doctrine of creation matters for the integration of psychology and Christianity. *Journal of Psychology and Theology, 48*(1). https://www.doi.org/10.1177/0091647119837024

Whitney, W. B., Dwiwardani, C., & Gonsalves, O. A. (2023). Why women's theological perspectives matter for teaching psychology. *Journal of Psychology and Christianity, 42*, 29-40.

Willard, D. (1998). *The divine conspiracy: Rediscovering our hidden life in God* (1st ed.). HarperSanFrancisco.

Williams, D. (2012). Black theology and womanist theology. In D. N. Hopkins & E. P. Antonio (Eds.), *The Cambridge companion to Black theology* (pp. 58-72). Cambridge University Press.

Winnicott, D. W. (1965). *The maturational processes and the facilitating environment.* Hogarth.

Wolf, A. (1992). Minorities in U.S. history textbooks, 1945–1985. *The Clearing House: A Journal of Educational Strategies, Issues and Ideas, 65*(5), 291-97. https://www.doi.org/10.1080/00098655.1992.10114228

Wolters, A. M. (2005). *Creation regained: Biblical basis for a reformational worldview.* Eerdmans.

Wolterstorff, N. (1984). *Reason within the bounds of religion.* Eerdmans.

Wolterstorff, N. (2009). *Lament for a son.* Eerdmans.

Woodley, R. (2008). North American native theology. In W. A. Dyrness & V. M. Kärkkäinen (Eds.), *Global dictionary of theology.* InterVarsity Press.

Wright, N. T. (2006). *Evil and the justice of God.* InterVarsity Press.

Wright, N. T. (2008). *Surprised by hope: Rethinking heaven, the resurrection, and the mission of the church.* HarperCollins.

Yangarber-Hicks, N., Behensky, C., Canning, S. S., Flanagan, K. S., Gibson, N. J. S., Hicks, M. W., Kimball, C. N., Pak, J. H., Plante, T., & Porter, S. L. (2006). Invitation to the table conversation: A few diverse perspectives on integration. *Journal of Psychology and Christianity, 25*(4), 338-53.

Yee, G. (2007). "She stood in tears amid the alien corn": Ruth the perpetual foreigner and model minority. In R. N. Brock (Ed.), *Off the menu: Asian and Asian North American women's religion and theology* (1st ed.) (pp. 45-68).Westminster John Knox.

Zurlo, G. A., Johnson, T. M., & Crossing, P. F. (2021). World Christianity and mission 2021: Questions about the future. *International Bulletin of Mission Research, 45*(1), 15-25. https://doi.org/10.1177/2396939320966220

Index

An Association for Christian Psychologists,
Therapists, Counselors and Academicians

CAPS is a vibrant Christian organization with a rich tradition. Founded in 1956 by a small group of Christian mental health professionals, chaplains and pastors, CAPS has grown to more than 2,100 members in the U.S., Canada and more than 25 other countries.

CAPS encourages in-depth consideration of therapeutic, research, theoretical and theological issues. The association is a forum for creative new ideas. In fact, their publications and conferences are the birthplace for many of the formative concepts in our field today.

CAPS members represent a variety of denominations, professional groups and theoretical orientations; yet all are united in their commitment to Christ and to professional excellence.

CAPS is a non-profit, member-supported organization. It is led by a fully functioning board of directors, and the membership has a voice in the direction of CAPS.

CAPS is more than a professional association. It is a fellowship, and in addition to national and international activities, the organization strongly encourages regional, local and area activities which provide networking and fellowship opportunities as well as professional enrichment.

To learn more about CAPS, visit www.caps.net.

The joint publishing venture between IVP Academic and CAPS aims to promote the understanding of the relationship between Christianity and the behavioral sciences at both the clinical/counseling and the theoretical/research levels. These books will be of particular value for students and practitioners, teachers and researchers.

For more information about CAPS Books, visit InterVarsity Press's website at www.ivpress.com/christian-association-for-psychological-studies-books-set.

Finding the Textbook You Need

The IVP Academic Textbook Selector
is an online tool for instantly finding the IVP books
suitable for over 250 courses across 24 disciplines.

ivpacademic.com